Early Pr...
Bearing It: 12 Women Find Resilience

These twelve women who have bravely shared their poignant and compelling stories represent the very best of us; their voices and stories deserve to be honored and recognized. I could not move from one chapter to the next without taking time to be still and reflect upon the magnitude of life experiences filling the pages. This book is a treasure trove of wisdom that comes from both the sorrows and joys of life. —Diane K. Anderson, PhD, Vice President for Student Affairs, Western Michigan University

In Lin-Manuel Miranda's musical *Hamilton*, one song describes Eliza and Alexander's grief after the death of their son as "too terrible to name" and "unimaginable." The twelve contributors to this book have also had to endure truly unimaginable trauma and loss. But in each of these honest essays, we learn about bravery, acceptance, and resilience. I admire these writers for their determination to move forward with purpose and hope. —Jennifer Grant, author of eight books for adults and children including *Dimming the Day: Evening Meditations for Quiet Wonder*, *Maybe God is Like that Too*, and *Finding Calm in Nature: A Guide for Mindful Kids*

This is an exceptional collection of stories demonstrating a true kaleidoscope of personalities, emotions, and fortitude in the face of tremendous challenges. Each story will challenge the reader to reflect on their own experiences in light of these dramatic personal narratives. A great read! —Gene Frost, MDiv, EdD, Executive Director, The Wheaton Academy Foundation, author of *Learning from the Best*

Bearing It reveals so much good and beauty in the human spirit. The courageous souls who share their personal stories of confronting challenges and disappointment have done so with uncommon grace and exceptional strength of character. Facing illness, suffering, and death is daunting. Yet, the vignettes in this extraordinary work provide us with illustrations of triumph. This book is a fount of hope. Its characters are truly exemplars for all time, exhorting us to fear not. While reading this book, I felt my spirit strengthen and love envelop me. I heard a still, small voice encourage me to take life head on and live every day to its fullest. This primer for life deserves to be on every nightstand. —Arnie Holtberg, former Headmaster, educational consultant, and author of *Game On!*

Mary Oliver once wrote, "I tell you this to break your heart, by which I mean only that it break open and never close again to the rest of the world." These inspiring stories of human suffering and strength will break your heart wide open, creating more room for compassion, love, and hope. A big thank you to every woman who courageously shared her story that showcased the beauty and brutality of the human experience. —Victoria Robb Powers, MDiv, senior minister, and author of *My Love, God Is Everywhere*

BEARING IT

Also by
Christine Nicolette-Gonzalez

My Mother's Curse:
A Journey Beyond Childhood Trauma

Bearing It:

12 Women Find Resilience

You Can Too

Compiled and Edited

by

Christine Nicolette-Gonzalez

LAUREATE
LIFE PRESS
Dallas

With deep love, this book is dedicated
to Analise, Sally, Ellie, and Aidy.
It was compiled with gratitude for
every woman who knows
she must keep fighting
for a better world.

Contents

Why This Book Was Written   1

Seasoned Perseverance   5
Tracey McKenzie

Thou Shalt Not Be Overcome   22
Jan Neece

On My Worst Day, There Was Room For Joy   32
Leslie McKinney

Reframing My Limited Life   68
Kerrin Rummel

Finding My Next Steps Forward   84
Julia L. Williams Dade

"Cry, Cry"   101
Leanne Mertzman

The Unhung Swing   120
Leslie Cechan

Chaos And Silence   142
Dinah Harris

The Power Of *Sankofa*   176
Kristene Ruddle

The Long Ride Home   197
Linda Dean McDermitt

In The Light Of The Moon   220
Layla Shah

Centered After All   235
Jan Quesada

Acknowledgments   259

WHY THIS BOOK WAS WRITTEN

It was November 30, 2021—my beautiful dog Aria's second birthday. I thought we would celebrate her special day in a large dog park just a few miles from my home. As I stood at the far end of the park, I smiled as I watched her romp with four other doodles that happened to be there that day. It was fun to talk to their owners and share some of the joys of raising our lively dogs. Suddenly, in the middle of a sentence, I found myself on the ground writhing in pain that came from the back of my right knee. When I looked up, I saw a large dog running away. The pain was so intense and reminded me of the pain in my left knee that I had experienced on the tennis court twenty years earlier. I soon learned that in this freak accident the dog had torn my right ACL and meniscus.

Why me?

Here it was, just a few weeks before the holiday season that I had been waiting so long for. Due to the pandemic, it had been two years since my growing family of nine had been together. So much had to be done to prepare for their arrival, but now in that one instant, all my plans seemed to die in the dust that covered my face.

Throughout my life, several of my friends have described me as a healthy, accomplished woman who is just quite unlucky and accident prone. As a child and young adult, I experienced trauma that no child should ever experience. In my adulthood, numerous accidents and surgeries have proven their words to be true.

Yes. Why me?

When I wrote my memoir that chronicled my childhood trauma, *My Mother's Curse: A Journey Beyond Childhood Trauma*, I wrote of learning to not ask "Why me?" but rather, "What for?"

Throughout my life, the "What for?" of my challenging childhood has been answered in numerous ways, the primary one being my ability to help many people, especially my students, as they deal with the significant challenges in their lives.

So as I sat healing from yet another injury, I began to think about the women I knew who could now inspire me with their resilience, women who were bearing tragedies far greater than recovering from a knee injury. And there were plenty of them:

- Jan had just completed her mastectomy, chemotherapy, and radiation for stage-three breast cancer; would it return?
- Leslie, a mother of two young girls, was reeling after losing her husband to ALS, having been his primary caregiver for over six years.
- Kerrin was in her thirteenth year of enduring chronic fatigue syndrome, which made it difficult for her to do any activity for longer than fifteen minutes at a time.
- Julia was still trying to understand the suicide of her twenty-three-year-old son.
- Linda was in her twenty-fifth year of caring for her daughter who was born with so many birth defects that she would always need fulltime care.
- Layla was at the end of her second abusive marriage and was trying to discern her best next steps as she would now be a single parent to her two sons, one with special needs.

And I had other friends who were bearing a much tougher hand of cards than I had been dealt. Their stories inspired me, and I suspected they would inspire other people, too. Yes, this resilient group of women that spanned four decades had so much to teach us about facing life's challenges.

In that moment, this book was born.

Through these women's stories, I've been reminded that sometimes I cannot control what happens to me, but I can change how I react to life's inevitable challenges. These stories reveal that we all have a choice: we can either take what has been dealt to us and allow it to make us better people who grow past our circumstances, or we can allow our circumstances to tear us down. We can realize that we don't have to be victims; rather, we can learn ways to not waste any of our suffering.

It is my hope and prayer that after reading these inspiring stories you also will be better equipped to bear whatever challenges you are facing right now or that you will inevitably face in the future.

Christine Nicolette-Gonzalez
2023

Seasoned Perseverance

Tracey McKenzie

"Whatever you do, don't try to move! You've been in a terrible car accident!"

The sturdy yet calming voice jolted me out of the empty darkness. Blurred white, yellow, and gray colors surrounded me and made the pounding in my head seem more extreme. The brisk fall wind smacked my face. My mind was frantically spinning, trying to remember what happened. Then I slowly sank back into a dark, empty void.

When I finally came to, I was temporarily blinded by the florescent flashing lights of the first responders' vehicles. The intense stench of burning flesh and the blood-curdling shrieks of terror resounded so loudly in my head that I couldn't think straight. *Where am I? What is happening?*

At that moment, I heard a voice in the distance cry out, "Oh my God, look at her!" *What did they mean, look at who? Me? What in the world was happening?*

Initially, all I could make out were blurred lights and greyish silhouettes moving in all directions. As my right eye came into focus, I realized that the car that I was a passenger in was intertwined with another vehicle. And I was a mutilated mess. *What's wrong with my left eye? Why can't I see anything out of it? Where is my date, Chris? What happened to him? Why can't I move?* Still strapped into the passenger seat covered in my own blood, I wanted so badly to see what was happening or at least to stop resisting the desire to rest my eyes in the darkness that seemed to be calling me.

As the Senior Class President of L.V. Berkner High School in Richardson, Texas, I was known as a reliable leader, honor roll student, and nationally ranked athlete. I never thought that anything catastrophic would happen to me. For the previous seventeen years, I had what seemed like the "good-luck golden touch." I seemed to excel at most things—all with a good attitude and a cheerful disposition. Never in a million years would I have believed that I would not be healthy and agile. I naively assumed I was indestructible and would stay youthful and energetic forever. I felt this way until 11:36 p.m. on Friday, October 26, 1989—the fall evening that changed my life forever.

Earlier that week, I had made the decision to attend a homecoming game of a rival school in the Dallas area with Chris, a childhood friend. He had recently endured a tough breakup with his longtime girlfriend, so he invited me to be his plus-one for his school's homecoming weekend. Little did we know what lay ahead and how that weekend would forever change our lives.

It is inconceivable that the excruciating trauma I endured that night obliterated my memory of the actual impact; however, I will never forget the fear in Chris' eyes when he looked at me after the accident. I can vividly remember the bright lights of the other cars that witnessed the accident, the horrific stench that filled the air, and the frantic screams from others who surrounded me. I don't remember the pain that my body endured. However, I do remember pondering how my Evan Picone pantyhose that my mother demanded that I purchase and wear to the game because "only loose women don't wear pantyhose," were utterly ruined. I do not remember how the sizzling metal of the car felt on my skin. However, I do remember the thickness of the blood that blanketed my body, my seemingly broken bones, and the huge chunks of flesh that seemed to adhere themselves to my black leather skirt and mustard yellow blouse. *For heavens sakes, this was my brand-new leather skirt, and now it's all ruined!*

As I sat there trying to determine what had happened, wrestling with either fighting to stay focused or closing my eyes to the darkness that called me, the deafening screams were a huge distraction. With my right eye, I forced myself to peer out of the shattered front car window. I saw Chris sitting on the cold pavement, moaning, while rocking back and forth. The vision of his body still haunts me.

~⁓~

The evening had begun with such great promise. We had a fun time watching the football game and interacting with mutual friends. After the game, Chris drove us to the neighborhood IHOP where we dined with a group of our friends. After our meal, we headed home. Chris was proudly driving his father's new car, and we were listening to "Miss You Much" by Janet Jackson. We gleefully sang with the windows rolled down and the sunroof pulled back, and we relaxed as we enjoyed the final part of our evening together.

Chris was driving forty-one miles per hour on the feeder road of the expressway. Smiling and bebopping to the music, he apparently failed to yield at a sign. Before he could even react, a royal blue Jeep Cherokee with its doors and rooftop unzipped and open departed the expressway and careened onto the exit ramp traveling at 118 miles per hour. The driver of the Jeep was drinking his ninth beer of the evening. His girlfriend sat gleefully in the passenger seat. Both were singing and dancing to deafening rock music. Beer cans filled the floor of their back seat. Laughter and singing could be heard from the Jeep. Until...until the Jeep collided with Chris' father's car.

Why can't I remember the impact? Did I doze off? Wasn't I enjoying the song on the radio? Maybe I was looking the other way. What happened to me? I couldn't remember the moment that the Jeep hit our car. I couldn't remember how the Jeep's force of impact allowed its hood to open and bend. How the Jeep's car battery had been catapulted out of the engine and barreled at full force through our front windshield, detonating when it struck my face. Clearly, I was caught by surprise.

I now realized that the burning flesh in my lap was the left side of my face. The only thing that remained on that side of my face was my left eyeball, and it dangled from the opening in my cracked skull.

I then realized that it was not just my face that was affected. I could not move, nor could I feel anything at all. I began to think seemingly irrational thoughts. *Why is everyone staring at me? Why isn't anyone helping me? This can't be real. This must be a horrendous nightmare.* I began to panic. *My breathing feels funny. Why can't I get up? Ugh! This is so incredibly frustrating.* I felt completely alone for a few minutes, which felt like years. *Maybe I'm paralyzed? Is that why I can't feel anything? Oh, God! What's happening? Oh wait, I feel something. Holy crap—this hurts!*

I eventually started to feel the shattered glass that was stuck to my torso and sprinkled throughout my skin. Then I felt blood sliding down my face, almost like large tears. I heard Chris' screams and watched him rush out of the car. He hastily sprinted to the passenger side of the car and pulled open the door. I watched the blood from my face smear onto his cold, shaking hands as he tried to get me out of the mangled car.

A woman stopped him and told him not to move me. *Who was she? Who told her to not let anyone help me? Doesn't this lady realize that I'm trapped and can't move?*

Despite my frustration, I somehow noticed that our glass-shattered window was scattered in pieces inside our car and on the side of the expressway. My blood, dripping onto my lap and seat, looked like melting ice cream on a sweltering summer day. After seeing the pools of blood covering my body, everything slowly faded to black again. I began to drift in and out of my dark and lonely place. *This actually isn't so bad. I can rest just for a while. Maybe they can wake me up whenever someone decides to come and help me.*

Suddenly, I felt a cold hand touching my right shoulder. A soft voice was calling my name. *Wake up, Tracey! Someone is calling you.* I desperately wanted to respond, but I couldn't. My mouth wouldn't work. There was a giant lump in my throat, like the feeling of dry swallowing a giant pill without any water, or the feeling of desperately trying to hold back tears. No matter how hard I tried, I couldn't speak.

The woman who told me not to move asked me for my home phone number. I held up my fingers and signed the number to her. Then she prayed with me. She told me to hold on and to not give up. She said that I was saved for a reason. Her voice was soft as she touched my hands. *I felt a flutter of hope in my heart.* She explained that she was going to contact my family. *Who was this angel of hope? She seemed so caring. Why can't I open my left eye? Why does everything seem so dark and scary? Why can't I stay focused?*

As I sat there trying desperately to stay awake, I noticed the crowd of people that were standing near the car grow larger in size. People were pointing at me and staring at the car. *What am I, a freak show? Why are you all pointing at me? Why won't someone help me? Why can't I keep my eyes open?*

Unknown to me, several of the onlookers were helping. When the drunk driver of the Jeep took off in a full sprint from the accident site, some onlookers chased him down, restrained him, and brought him back to the accident site. While his girlfriend's leg was caught between our two cars, one onlooker had already called 911.

Help was on the way. *It's so dark. I want to close my eyes and just fall asleep. I feel so tired, so lonely, so cold.*

After what seemed like an eternity, I recognized the sounds of sirens. I worked hard to open my right eye. I could hear the sirens getting louder and closer. I could vaguely make out uniforms, loud voices of authority, and louder sirens. Before I could tell who was nearby, a lady bent down next to me and whispered softly in my ear, "Help is here. Hang on beautiful. The first responders are here to save you!" *Ah! My angel lady. You are so kind.*

Soon I could hear the ambulances, a team of paramedics giving orders, the firefighters getting their equipment out, and other people moving at a rapid pace. Sirens blared in the background. The jaws of life were used to cut the drunk drivers' girlfriend out from between the two contorted vehicles. The loud noise of the hustle and bustle kept me from falling further into my dark place. As I waited, I tried to focus and stay calm.

After many long minutes, I heard a loud voice say, "We're here sweetheart. Hang on! We'll get you out of here." Finally. The cavalry had come. The first responders seemed kind and resolved as they cut me out from the mangled passenger car seat.

At that moment, I heard a voice that sounded familiar. I strained to open my right eye. In the distance I could see my father running toward me at full sprint, screaming in agony at the sight of my mutilated body. My angel lady must have reached my family. *Holy crap! Is that my daddy? Is he really running? I had never seen my daddy run before. Something must be terribly wrong! Am I dead?*

It was then that I realized I was still alive. I saw a look of anguish on my father's face. And then I blacked out.

The doctors later told my parents that the entire time that I was in the car, my body had been in shock—which turned out to have saved my life. But once I came out of shock, I lost consciousness. The paramedics worked swiftly to care-flight me to Baylor Hospital in downtown Dallas, one of the largest hospitals in the Dallas area, while Chris, the drunk driver, and his girlfriend were all transported to a smaller, nearby hospital.

After about twenty minutes in the air, our helicopter arrived at the landing pad on the hospital roof. I was quickly rushed into the building and wheeled to the operating area to be prepped for surgery. While there, I remember the overhead lights burning so brightly that they made me nauseated. I remember needing to use the restroom but not being able to communicate that to anyone around me.

Should I use it here on this cold stainless-steel table? Of course, I shouldn't. Ladies don't pee on tables in public! I may be hurt, but I'm not dead. My mom would kill me if I used the bathroom on myself, and in public no less!

My thoughts were interrupted by the loud sounds of people running and doctors and nurses speaking loudly and asking me questions. *Don't these people know that I can't move my mouth to talk? Why are they talking to me? What I need is some privacy so that I can use the bathroom in peace!*

My thoughts turned quickly to the sound of nearby wailing.

I kept working feverishly to open my right eye. Finally, through my hazy vision, I made out the shapes of my parents standing near my lifeless body, howling in despair and praying for a miracle. My mother, with rollers in her hair, was wearing a coat to conceal her nightgown and gold house slippers. *I can't believe that my mother is breaking her own rule of being presentable in a public space. Oh, my heavens. What she's wearing is almost scandalous!*

My father was wearing one of the first responder's jackets and his boxer shorts. *Oh, my! Everyone in the world has lost their minds today. I can't believe that Daddy is standing in front of people in his plaid boxer shorts!* While grabbing for my mangled left hand, Daddy seemed to be trying to contain his emotions. The pastor of our church was standing with my parents providing words of comfort and Scripture to hold close to their hearts. *Well, at least he was fully dressed.*

It seemed to take a long time before the three exhausted souls were asked to leave the operating room so the doctors could begin their work. A doctor placed his hands on my forehead and asked me to count backwards from ten. *Of course, I can do that. This is easy. Ten, nine, eight...* before I knew it, I was knocked out, ready to fight for my life yet again.

A vast team of surgeons worked tirelessly for *seventeen* hours to save my life. My list of injuries was long and complex. I suffered from a compound fractured skull, several broken ribs, a severely lacerated liver, pelvic bruises, and burns to my body. The surgeons had used hundreds of stitches to put my mangled body and face back together. In addition to these procedures, most of the left side of my face was missing. It had been burned off. The doctors grafted skin from the back of my thighs to replace the skin on my face. *Finally, my big backside was being useful.*

The initial days in the hospital ICU were a matter of survival. The left side of my body was immobile as I was unable to move muscles in my face, my leg, or even lift my arm. My fractured cranium and the left side of my face were severely swollen by the trauma from the battery's impact and detonation. Innumerable stitches held my face together. My nearly severed optical nerve and left eyeball were wrapped up completely by gauze and bandages.

During my second night in the ICU, after regaining consciousness, I intentionally strained to glance around my hospital room. I needed to see where I was and what was happening. The room was dark, and the only dim lights seemed to be in a far corner near the door. My parents were both sleeping in the hard-backed chairs near the window on the right side of the room. There were masses of flowers and balloons with attached cards that covered the counter tops and mobile hospital tray. The door of my room was closed, but the left side of the room looked strange. *Wait, what is that? Is that a sheet over the mirror? Why did they cover up the bathroom mirror? What do I look like? Oh, my stars in heaven…what is wrong with me?*

After ten prolonged days and nights that seemed to run together, it was finally revealed to me why the mirror was covered. The swelling of my skull and face caused my face to look extremely unbalanced and disfigured. The team of doctors did not want my initial response to my physical appearance to derail my emotional state and the initial days of my physical therapy.

As the days passed, my parents began to take shifts staying with me. The steady stream of visitors and friends who once came in droves to see me lessened and then disappeared completely. My fellow cheerleaders and high school friends stopped coming by as often. Soon my insecurities grew louder as my connection to others began to unravel.

Would I ever look the same? Will I be ugly and disfigured forever? Will I be able to walk without a limp, move quickly, or even laugh without pain? Will anyone ever want to spend time with me again?

Loneliness, sadness, and anger began to fill my mind.

One afternoon, my day nurse, Nurse G., came in to give me my medication. She politely asked me how I was doing. Although my speech was not clear, my sobs and anguished sounds of misery were as apparent as the physical scars on my body. *Why was this happening to me? My "perfect" life was over. I wasn't the one drinking and driving. I was just a passenger minding my own business and living my best teenage life. Why me?*

My wailing was loud, but my physical and emotional pain was louder. My sobs shook my body and intensified the pain. I was angry. I was depressed. I couldn't speak phrases yet, so talking to anyone was not an option. I had always been a talker. I was always the life of the party. Yet here I was now. I felt useless, lonely, and hopeless. I felt as though the battery that exploded in my face had blown my entire world to smithereens. *Here I am all bandaged up, and where is that drunk driver? He's probably out happily living his life going about his daily duties. Meanwhile, my life is turned upside down.*

Nurse G. instinctively knew how to assist me without asking any other questions. She came over to me and just held me as my now ninety-five-pound body collapsed in her arms from hopelessness, exhaustion, and depression. She let me cry until I couldn't cry any longer.

Then, she took my bandaged face in her hands and said, "You are allowed to scream. You are allowed to cry. But you are not allowed to give up! God saved you for a reason. Be the reason for someone else by living your best life!"

As she said those words, I felt another flutter in my heart. Her simple act of compassion did so much to bolster my self-control and self-esteem. I knew what she said was right. Just like my angel lady had said, for some reason, I had been saved. I could not give up. I needed to keep living.

~~~

Over the course of the next six months, I endured eight painful surgeries to fix my body, four oral surgeries to fix my mouth and jaw, hundreds of hours of counseling and physical therapy to learn how to walk and talk again, and excruciating pain that at times torched my soul. Despite the hard days, I could finally see some light at the end of the tunnel. My hard work on my physical and mental state was paying off; I was healing.

Then I found out that the drunk driver was still evading arrest and charges in regard to the accident. *How could this be? Why wasn't he getting what he deserved?!* I was angry and frustrated; however, I realized that I needed to move past those emotions if I was going to heal. I needed to let go of my anger towards the drunk driver. I needed to forgive my friends whom I thought should have been standing with me in solidarity as I healed. I needed to recognize them for what they were—young teenagers who were trying to live their own lives as best as they possibly could. I needed to forgive myself for "letting this happen to me." I needed to allow my healing process to take its time. And through my healing, I learned two important skills: perseverance and grit.

During March, nearly five months later, my doctors, physical therapists, nurses, and countless other medical professionals challenged me to dig deep, focus, and persevere. Within weeks, I left the hospital and headed home.

Then more challenges began as I learned to navigate my childhood home in new ways. I learned to be patient with my physical limitations and at times fragile mental state. I learned to rest in the darkness each night. Initially, I was afraid to close my eyes as the flashbacks of the accident were often debilitating. I was scared that something else horrific would happen to me or that I might not wake up. The anxiety that I had developed over the past six months was frequently crippling; however, I had to deal with it one moment at a time.

Although I had spent most of my senior year in the hospital, my teachers worked with my parents and me on my academic credits. Their kindness allowed me the opportunity to graduate with my senior class.

On Friday, May 25, 1990, as the Senior Class President, I was charged to give the address to our graduating class. Months of physical, speech, and emotional therapy to recover my abilities and fortitude had paid off. Standing before my class, I honored the wonderful "angels" who had inspired me to keep working hard and not to quit—the strong women who cared enough to pour their blessings and prayers into me. Because of them, my family, the doctors, therapists, and nurses, I was able to stand on my own, walk across the stage in front of thousands, give the graduation address, graduate, and celebrate with my class. Just a few months later, I was even able to attend a college close to my home.

～～

From that tragic event, my life story became one of learning how to deal with the unthinkable every day and rebounding with joy and grace. The accident traumatized me. I should have been dead. Due to my many scars, my ego and self-esteem were destroyed. I had always been a person who thrived on being popular and who enjoyed a deep connection with others. Watching others judge or avoid me when I didn't look as beautiful as I once did really shook me. I had to dig deep and find joy within myself instead of in the tons of friends whom I thought I had. I had to do the hard work of being gutted from all that I knew physically and rebuild myself both literally and figuratively. There were days where I felt lonely and depressed. There were days when my physical pain seemed too much to bear. There were days when I allowed the depths of my unthinkable trauma and helplessness get the best of me.

However, when those days came around, I thought about my two angels—my angel lady at the scene of the accident and Nurse G. who both reminded me that I was saved so that I could live. They reminded me that despite my current situation, my life was still worth living. Their selflessness and compassion inspired me to continue to work hard to live regardless of the pain, loneliness, and physical and mental scars that I bore. Their words were a balm to my soul, and they still inspire me today.

Since that fateful year, I graduated from college and graduate school and have had several fulfilling careers. I married and went through the joys of bringing two beautiful children into this world. I have developed true friendships with other women, and we have stood by one another without fail. I have been a victim of emotional and physical abuse where once again my self-esteem and physical wellbeing were tested to unbearable limits and plummeted.

Despite the bad days and challenges that have shaken me to my core, I still remember my angel ladies. Trouble doesn't always last. Because of their guidance during the most challenging experience of my life, I've been able to apply their words as I've navigated through other gut-wrenching and soul-snatching experiences. Their soothing words were the best medicine for my numerous scars and injuries.

For a while, my disfigured face was the hardest for my ego to shake. The human face represents who we are and how people perceive us. It also contains many of the primary ways that we interact with the world through sight, sound, smell, and taste. I endured physical and emotional distress long after the accident due to the scarring and my disfigurement. There were many days that I felt broken, depressed, and alone.

However, despite my pain and scars, I always remembered what my two angels said to me. I remembered how they were there for me when no one else was. I remembered how they were patient, calm, and resolute in their encouragement. I remember the flutters in my heart when they spoke those words of encouragement. Their words helped me realize that I was saved. I was still alive—alive to tell my story.

~

Today, thirty-three years later, I still suffer from the injuries that I sustained on that catastrophic evening. During these past years, I have had a great deal of plastic and maxillofacial surgery to fix my facial scarring. Amazing dental specialists have performed various procedures to reduce pain, fix deformities, and restore function to my lower face. To this day, my body still aches whenever the weather changes, when the air conditioning is too high, or sometimes for seemingly no reason at all. But through it all, what has kept me going is the thought that *I am still here.*

Thanks to my angel ladies, I am determined to become all that I can be—not settling for becoming just a fraction of the vibrant young woman that I was. I am a go-getter, a fighter, and a survivor. I have purpose, strength, and vitality. I have a great family and many friends who love me despite my internal and external scars. My angel ladies were right—I was spared for a reason.

I started a collection of angel figurines in 1990, and I'm still collecting them. Because of the gentle yet powerful words of my two angels, I have survived and thrived. I am now a happily remarried mother of five with two precious adult children and three amazing bonus adult children. I'm also an educator, author, and advocate for many causes. I am so grateful to have survived the terror of what I've been through as it has given me perspective when helping others to live their best lives. I truly believe that I was spared so that I could encourage others to survive and thrive through whatever horrific circumstances might come their way. I am grateful. I am hopeful. And despite my many sins and scars, I am proud of my journey.

I should have died. Yet, I survived. I listened and learned through the flutters of my heart.

THOU SHALT NOT BE OVERCOME

JAN NEECE

On Christmas Day, 2019, I woke up early and excited. Like over twenty Christmases before, my husband, children, and I were in the comfortable Kentucky home of my parents. Their neat brick rancher, with its green carpet and warm wood furniture, had not been updated in years, which made it seem familiar. Though I had not lived in Kentucky for thirty-five years, my parents' home was still a haven, a place where my roots ran deep.

With Christmas lights twinkling and homey decorations in every corner, I felt incredibly thankful for my life. I was married to John, a sweet and funny man whom I deeply admired and loved. My grown daughter Faith was working in the Episcopal Service Corps in Harrisburg, Pennsylvania. My son Bennett was in his final year at the University of Tennessee. We would soon gather around a table with my eighty-six-year-old parents, my sister, brother-in-law, and nephews.

I reflected on what a beautiful year it had been. There had been opportunities earlier in 2019 to vacation to where we used to live in Texas and to see family and friends in Dallas and San Antonio. For the first time in twenty-five years, my husband and I returned to the campus of Texas A&M where we had met and fallen in love. I had also made time that summer to see some dear friends I had worked with at the University of Georgia over thirty years before. Just a few weeks before Christmas, I was honored when I received an award as Hospital Provider of the Year at the children's hospital in Knoxville, Tennessee, where I serve as Director of Pediatric Psychology Services. It was the first time my physician colleagues had honored a psychologist, and I was deeply grateful. Over a seven-year period, our department had grown from a one-woman office to a multi-person staff, and I anticipated more growth in the year ahead.

While visiting my parents' home that Christmas, I noticed something different about the appearance of my right breast. I could not feel a lump, but it seemed that my bra was leaving marks on my skin that were different than the other breast. I thought maybe I just needed a new bra. But I also had a sneaky feeling that maybe I needed a mammogram. It had been a little over a year since my last one.

So in mid-January, I had a routine mammogram. At that time, a nurse practitioner did a breast exam and said things looked okay. She told me that we could do an ultrasound, but since she said she didn't think it was necessary, I chose not to have it. That afternoon, I celebrated by going to Soma to get a fitting and buying a couple of pretty new bras.

By March, however, my breast still looked different. Even worse, I could feel something unusual when I pressed down on it. I made an appointment with my PCP, and she could feel something different, too. This time she asked the mammogram clinic to do an advanced screening.

That week in March 2020 was a scary one for the entire country. The coronavirus was not going away, and it quickly became clear that big changes in every line of work were going to be required. As the director of four pediatric psychologists at a children's hospital in Knoxville, Tennessee, we see some patients in the hospital, some in multidisciplinary clinics, and some in our own outpatient office. After a couple of weeks of speculation, the word had come that our practice—and every other specialty office associated with the hospital—would have to change our procedures. We scrambled to get telehealth up and running so we could help our patients without putting them and ourselves at risk for Covid.

On the day of the mammogram screening, I was scared as I sat in a different room than the one I had sat in just two months earlier. This higher-risk room was very quiet and somber. The colors seemed bluer. The ambient music sounded creepy rather than comforting, and the air was colder.

And this time, the mammogram took much longer. An ultrasound was also performed. Afterwards, a frowning nurse told me, "The doctor is coming soon. You need to know it's bad news. I'll give you a moment to absorb this so you can listen closely to the doctor's recommendations."

It's strange how well I recall that nurse's words. But the only words I remember the doctor saying were "cancer" and "aggressive."

There were a few more tests done that day, including lymph node tissue sampling. It was a life-altering afternoon. I had never faced anything as scary as this before.

Yes, at earlier times, I had undergone some medical tests that were concerning in the sense that I *could* have gotten bad news. But there hadn't been bad news for the heart test or the thyroid nodule biopsy that were conducted in my fifties. In 2015, I faced several weeks of recovery after our sweet but rambunctious dog pulled me off our porch, and I was suddenly on the ground looking down at a bone sticking out where my ankle was supposed to be. But I had recovered from that injury without significant complications, and my life had not been endangered by that compound fracture.

My husband is also a psychologist, and he and I only call each other during work hours if we have an emergency. This certainly was one. John cancelled the rest of his day and drove to be with me while I was still at the mammogram center. I had not asked him to come immediately because there was nothing he could do. But I will always be grateful that he came as fast as he could just to hold my hand and cry with me.

The next few weeks were a blur of activity that seemed to happen both in slow motion and not fast enough. I did not have faith in the facility where the mammogram was done nor in their associated medical team. I kept wondering if an ultrasound in January would have picked up what was more obvious in March. After many phone calls, we found a different medical team that agreed to work with me. And I began my journey with three bright, lovely women who would fight my cancer with me—an oncologist, a surgeon, and a radiologist.

The first woman I met was the oncologist. Due to her facemask, I could only see half of her face, and she could only see half of mine. She pulled no punches about the aggressiveness of my breast cancer—

unfortunately, the Stage 3 type. But she also told my nervous husband and me, "Listen. This cancer is treatable." And I saw in her eyes that she meant it. She had confidence that I could be healed. For the first time in a few weeks, my husband and I dared to smile. We finally had a treatment plan.

Breast cancer treatment varies depending upon many factors: the size of the tumor, the cancer type, and whether it has escaped the breast and metastasized. For me, the treatment involved chemotherapy, surgery, and radiation, in that order.

I started my chemo treatments in April 2020. Over a sixteen-week period, I had four rounds of one type of chemo, then four rounds of a different type of chemo.

The scariest part of getting chemo in 2020 was the waiting room. It was filled with a couple dozen masked people keeping at least a seat apart from one another, not talking, but making guesses about the kind of cancer we were each dealing with. Once I was called back to the chemo chair, there was always a talkative nurse whose smile I could not see but felt. She drew the curtains and created a cocoon of sorts.

In the meantime, my work life was changing dramatically. Our children's hospital's IT team and other support staff and administrators pulled off a miracle in making telehealth a reality. I was able to take a laptop home and learned to use a special kind of Zoom to have confidential meetings with my patients. I had been reluctant to try telehealth before the pandemic hit, but now it was our only option. My husband's community health agency was also making telehealth an option for their practitioners and patients.

For sixteen weeks, I thought in terms of two-week spans. I would miss work to get chemo on the first Thursday of the cycle, I worked on Friday while I still felt good, then I took off the following Monday. I would feel sick and extremely fatigued over the weekend and into Monday. But by Tuesday, I could work again and would work the rest of the week and then the following Monday, Tuesday, and Wednesday.

I was fortunate to be able to work eight days out of every two weeks. In fact, my work was actually a tremendous blessing. Seeing my patients—children and teens with a range of issues, and the adults who cared for them—kept me from staying fixated on my own challenges.

But then it happened—I lost my hair. I had always had really thick hair, and it was so tough to watch it start to come out in clumps. Eventually, my husband helped me shave my head, and we laughed about the fact that I finally understood what it is like to be bald—he had been bald since his twenties. But I cried about losing my hair, too, as it always had been such an important part of my appearance.

Through it all, Covid hovered over us like fog. We ordered groceries for pick-up or delivery. In the summer of 2020, no one knew that it was pointless to wash groceries, so the grocery bags would go straight to the sink and counter. I washed milk cartons, sprayed down counters, and wiped cans. We worried about our supply of paper towels, wipes, toilet paper, and countless other things. Would they last?

The news seemed to be about nothing but the pandemic. More and more people were ending up in ICUs and dying. The greatest risks were to people like me—people over sixty and in poor health or with a compromised immune system. I could not stand the idea of ending up in an ICU without my husband and children at my side. I thought I could accept dying from cancer—but not from Covid. I was extremely cautious about masking, seeing others in closed spaces, and hugging anyone but my husband.

During this time, my children were also coping with the impact of the pandemic and having a mother who was fighting cancer. My daughter, who was working in Pennsylvania, learned that her work had to be done virtually, so she endured terrible loneliness. It was not safe for her to come home to visit us. We talked on the phone and did Zoom meetings, but it was no substitute for seeing each other in person. In July, my husband helped her move to Lexington, Kentucky, where she began new work and was able to share an apartment with a close friend; thankfully, this eased some of her isolation.

My son was finishing his final semester of college and living with several other young men in a house near campus. With a few weeks left in the semester, he decided to move home with us because all his classes had moved to virtual learning. His sweet girlfriend went to live with her parents in Memphis. He knew he could not socialize with anyone in person for awhile if he was staying with us. By mid-June, he had a new job and a new apartment. After he moved out of our home, we socialized by sitting outside, many feet apart, around a fire pit.

My dear parents in their upper eighties who still lived about three hours away in Kentucky couldn't visit us. Neither could my sister, brother-in-law, and nephews who also lived in Kentucky. Just when I could have used hugs the most, I couldn't get any! We talked on the phone and over Zoom, but once again, it was no replacement for the comfort given through physical touch.

Thankfully, I still felt the love and support of my family. I never doubted it. Their words of love, their prayers, and a tangible sense of their support seemed to make up for what we could not safely do in person.

The second step of my treatment, surgery, came in August. The second woman who helped me so much was the oncology surgeon. She listened well—usually rare in a surgeon—spoke frankly, but she also inspired great hope. I opted to have a bilateral mastectomy because the chance of my cancer showing up in my left breast was one in three. I had recently learned that I had a Chek-2 mutation that made those odds higher than average.

I opted to "go flat" and not do reconstructive surgery. This was a hard decision. I did not want to have yet another procedure to deal with, and I especially did not want to take the chance of altering the work of the radiation that was to come.

I was off work for two weeks following the mastectomy. But after two weeks, seeing patients again via telehealth was a huge blessing. Again, I could focus on someone other than just myself.

It was very strange to see myself without breasts. A nurse practitioner at the surgery office said, "The topography of your chest has changed, but you will come to appreciate its beauty."

She was right. I gradually felt tenderness, compassion, and gratitude when I looked at my flat chest. How fortunate it is to live at a time in history where a surgery like this could be done successfully! I was also blessed to have access to a great shop to help me with prosthetics and undergarments.

29

The third phase of my treatment, radiation, was yet another new endeavor. The final wonderful woman who guided me through this process was the oncology radiologist, a soft-spoken woman who had a straight-forward approach to cancer. I teased her that she "radiated" confidence, and she said that was her purpose.

Over six weeks, I had thirty radiation procedures. Thankfully, from the time I left home until I was back on a computer doing telehealth took less than an hour each day. Working throughout the radiation phase kept me focused on the bigger picture. I surely knew I wasn't the only person facing difficult circumstances that autumn.

The highlight of 2020 was getting my first Covid vaccine shot in mid-December. What a joy it was to be back at the hospital where I worked to receive an immunization!

By mid-January, 2021, I was back working in my office. We still saw many patients via telehealth, but now I also could meet with them in my office and see my colleagues in person again. Once again, my work provided such a healthy outlet for my recovery to continue.

Once my treatment was complete, I began taking a medication to lower the estrogen level in my body, since my particular cancer was sensitive to estrogen. And then several months later, I began taking an additional medication that has been shown to lower the risk of cancer's reoccurrence. Miraculously, my body has handled these medications without the difficult side effects that sometimes occur.

Throughout the experience of facing cancer, my deep faith in God sustained me. Scripture reading and engaging in centering prayer were practices that also kept me grounded. God showed me that my suffering was not meaningless. A quote by Julian of Norwich, an author from the Middle Ages, resonated with me: "[God] said not, 'Thou shalt not be tempested, thou shalt not be travailed, thou shalt not be diseased;' but he said, 'Thou shalt not be overcome.'"

I have also been helped by reading more about Acceptance and Commitment Therapy (ACT), a type of behavioral therapy that encourages mindfulness and acceptance of difficult feelings as well as living by one's values.

Most importantly, I was able to heal because of my relationships with my caring family members and friends. During 2020, I reconnected with several friends and distant family members I had not communicated with in years. I was amazed at how a text, an email, or a package would arrive just when I needed it most.

Another survivor of breast cancer said to me early on: "I may die of cancer someday, but that day is not today." There is so much wisdom in those words! I repeat her words every morning. At the time of this writing, I have had over 800 days to make choices about how to think about my cancer. I can spend all my mental energy thinking about whether my cancer will recur, or I can ask myself what I am called to do for that day. So far, I have not felt called to worry, to spend all day doing internet searches on breast cancer survivors, or to seek out statistics about the ways I will likely die. But I *have* felt called to accept the fact that I will die someday, and that knowledge has led me to live more intentionally with purpose each day.

ON MY WORST DAY, THERE WAS ROOM FOR JOY

LESLIE MCKINNEY

I don't want to be resilient. Nobody *wants* to be resilient. "Resilient" is what you're called only if you go through something really challenging. I don't know what the options are if you're not resilient. I may be resilient, but I'm also broken and sad. I don't know where to start, so I'm going to start with today.

Today I'm looking at my husband Forrest who looks like he's wrapped in bubble wrap, or at least that's what I see when I look at him. He's quadriplegic, which means that his body doesn't go anywhere on purpose; someone must put it there. And trying to keep the human body comfortable and in the right place when it doesn't want to move, and it has no means of correcting itself, is a difficult task.

Forrest is wearing a neck brace to keep his head from falling over. He has a strap around his chest to hold him in his chair and to keep him from sliding or falling forward. He has pads on each of his elbows to keep sores from forming. He has splints on both his hands to separate his fingers and keep his hands from curling up on themselves causing his nails—that grow far too quickly now—to dig into his hands. He has a belt around his waist to keep his hips from sliding forward and his rear as far back in his chair as it can stay.

Did I mention he's in a wheelchair? It's a power wheelchair—one that I control from the back as I drive him around our house or move him from location to location. A wheelchair that costs almost $80,000 and has more bells and whistles and tilts and mechanisms than you would even think possible. He lives in it almost all day.

On his legs he has compression bandages to keep edema from causing them to swell terribly from sitting all day long. Being quadriplegic doesn't help your circulation. He also has boots on his feet to help keep his heels from forming sores where they rest on the foot plates of his wheelchair. Along with this, there is a pillow behind his calves on his right side because he leans to the right, and this helps him stay pushed back, and a pillow behind his head. It's quite a sight when he's all wrapped in his "bubble wrap." It takes a lot of work to get a man who is 6'2" and not a little guy into that position.

I look over at him when I finish getting him set up for the day. I'm sweating and out of breath. He smiles up at me. His smile says what his voice cannot—*Thank you.*

Forrest hasn't spoken verbally in over five years.

From 2016 to 2022 Forrest and I shared our journey with ALS on Facebook as a way to share information, seek support/encouragement, and to give a glimpse into the complexities of life with a debilitating terminal illness. Everything shared was approved by Forrest with the hope that it may bring understanding, wisdom, and hopefully some good humor to anyone who would read them. This story highlights some of those posts.

LESLIE: AUGUST 15, 2016

Facebook friends, I want to let you all know that Forrest was admitted into the hospital yesterday. You may remember that in May he was hospitalized for pulmonary embolisms. Those were the result of medication he was taking because of fatigue he had been experiencing since the beginning of the year. Along with the fatigue, he started having slurred speech around March of this year. The speech and fatigue have only worsened in the last few months. Around July, he started having some weakness in his legs. He has been working with a specialist these last several months to address the symptoms and identify the root cause.

This past Friday he noticed that a portion of the vision in his right eye was missing. He was able to get in with an ophthalmologist Monday who diagnosed him as having ischemic optic neuropathy. He ordered some blood work which showed an increase in the inflammation indicators in the blood. Several doctors believed that it was vital for Forrest to go inpatient in the hospital to receive high doses of steroids to decrease inflammation with the hope that some of his vision would be restored. They also felt that his overall conditions were worsening instead of improving, and being in-patient would allow them to fast-track some tests so that they could diagnose and treat him quicker.

And that's where we are now. He has had two doses of the steroids and has seen some improvement in his vision and is overall feeling a little better.

Today the results of a spinal MRI indicated that the weakness in his legs and dropping of his foot was due to a pinched nerve. This appears to be a separate issue from the slurred speech and eye problem.

They still do not know what the underlying cause of those things are, but several things have been ruled out, and we both feel that he is getting the highest level of care. It feels like an episode of the TV show *House* at times. He has the student team assigned to him, and several specialists are interested in his case and are on a mission to figure this out.

LESLIE: NOVEMBER 2, 2016

Dear Facebook Friends and Family,

This is a VERY long post. Please bear with me.

Last week Forrest and I went to his neurologist and got the results of his muscle and nerve biopsies. I'm going to share the information that we have at this time to the best of my understanding and with the hopes that you will continue to pray/send positive thoughts for Forrest and our family. But I'm also going to give a good deal of information in case you, or someone you know, sees this post and may have some insight.

The results of the biopsy showed some axonal neuropathy and some myopathy but not severe enough to indicate a cause. The neurologist was looking for vasculitis, but none was found in that sample. Once again, the test results yielded more questions than answers. We also learned at this appointment that the results of blood work sent to the Mayo Clinic did not reveal any additional insight or information. While all of this should be comforting, the lack of a diagnosis was heartbreaking and frustrating.

Forrest's Current Status:

He is having a great deal of pain in his back. Pain has not been part of his symptoms until this last month. Through MRIs we know that he has a pinched nerve in his back which is the likely cause of his pain. He also had a large dose of steroids and has been weaning off of them for the past two months which is also probably why he has increased pain. In the last month he has been able to work but cannot do many of his normal activities of daily living. Getting showered/dressed used to take him thirty minutes. It took an hour and a half yesterday morning due to the pain in his back, severe fatigue, and general weakness. He is focused on continuing to work and help care for the girls. (For those of you who are new Facebook friends, Sophie is three now, and Violette is two.) He does not have the stamina or energy to do things like feed the dog, take out the trash, or do the dishes like he used to.

Next week he will be assessed for speech therapy again, physical therapy, and occupational therapy. We believe insurance will cover the PT because of the pinched nerve, but they have denied his speech therapy in the past because he did not have a cause for his dysarthria. The hope is that he can regain some strength and endurance, learn tools to help manage daily tasks, get some relief from the pain, and improve his speech.

Last week he also started a medication typically used for patients who have myasthenia gravis. Although this condition does not seem to apply to Forrest, the thought is that it couldn't hurt to try. I asked if we were just going to start throwing crap at this thing and see if anything sticks, and the doctor said, "Basically, yes." So far, this medication has not yielded any noticeable positive changes.

The next step, and we are in the process of working with insurance for approval, is an immunoglobulin therapy, IVIG. This comes with risks and the possibility of good success. But getting insurance to cover this expensive treatment without a definitive diagnosis may be difficult. He is also in the process of being referred to UT Southwestern for evaluation.

Symptoms:

In March, 2016, Forrest began to notice some changes in his speech—which were not noticeable to me or others—and general fatigue. He started with a new internist later that month. He was put on a regimen to help his energy. By mid-April his speech changes were significant and noticeable to me and his coworkers. His doctor started the process of having him evaluated by a neurologist. There were no indications of stroke or clear neurological causes. A brain MRI was completed. It was a healthy scan with no obvious cause for his speech issue. After this hospitalization, the speech issues continued, and he started noticing some weakness in both legs and dropping of his left foot. He fell twice between May and his next hospitalization in August. On September 26, 2016, he was hospitalized for four days for the muscle and nerve biopsy.

Tests that have been conducted:

MRI of brain, 3

MRA

Lumbar puncture

EMG

Cervical, thoracic and spinal MRI's

Countless blood tests

Countless neurological tests

CT scans of chest and head

Physicians who have been consulted:

Neurologist, ongoing

Hematologist, inpatient

Rheumatologist, inpatient

Internist, ongoing

If you pray:

Please pray for a diagnosis or reversal of his symptoms. No insurance obstacles for treatments. Quick entry into UT Southwestern program. Energy and pain management.

What we want you to know:

In addition to all the above, our life has joy, bad jokes, irritations, game nights, dinners together, and a great deal of love. Forrest was able to come to our fall festival at church, and while he couldn't walk around with the kids, he was able to sit where he could see them, and they could run back and forth between him and activities. He looks great if you were just to see him, but if he spoke or moved around too much you would see his limitations.

We are overwhelmed by our current conditions, but we are also filled with gratitude and love. We are sustained by your prayers and energies. In the midst of a very dark time, there is still a great deal of light. We are thankful to each of you and the roles you have played that have carried us through this time. We are incredibly thankful that Forrest's employer has been so supportive and allowed him to adjust his schedule as he has wrestled with new symptoms and limitations. I have never known a harder worker.

Despite all that has happened this year, the only workdays he has missed were when he was in the hospital. We don't know what time off he may need in the future, and he wants to keep being there for his team and keep his projects moving forward. We will keep doing life, even if we need to make some adjustments.

We are sharing all of this because we know how much you all care, and we want to keep you posted. But I have shared so much detail with the hopes that maybe you or someone you know may have some insight, want a case study, or could point us to a possible treatment. If you think you might be able to help and want any additional information, please do not hesitate to reach out.

Thanks again. All our love.

FORREST: JUNE 26, 2017

I have never been very active on Facebook. I am a classic Lurker. I check in from time to time to get the latest updates on friends and family. I love to see what is going on in your lives, look at your latest pictures, laugh at your jokes, and know more about your lives.

I am just not good about sharing my stories. I have always been that way. Luckily, I married an amazing woman, Leslie Bright McKinney, who is great at communicating and enjoys sharing moments and stories.

All that being said, there is major change and struggle in my and my family's life right now, and Leslie Bright McKinney has been sharing updates and extending thank yous on our behalf.

The amount of love and support being shown to me and my family is amazing. I have always been blessed to have each of you in my life.

39

Right now, I am blown away from the amount of love and support being shown to our family.

The words of encouragement, the well wishes, the amazing prayers, the financial support, the wonderful meals, the offers of help with activities for the girls, and every kind word of encouragement given to us—I cannot say thank you enough.

Many of you who have been aware of what is going on have asked along the way how you could help. We truly haven't known how best to answer this, as whatever "this" is, is unknown, and so that makes our future needs unknown. Now that things have progressively gotten worse, we do know some current needs, and some future things to prepare for so we can better respond to your gracious offers of time, money, meals, etc.

A lot of you wanted to help with the daunting financial burden. Again, we didn't know how to respond. I want to thank Joe Hill, Jill Valentine Hill, Phil Keith, and Kelley Harrison Keith for knowing what to do and setting up the Go Fund Me site for us to allow people to help that way. I am blown away by your generous financial gifts. It is appreciated so much.

I also can't say enough about my employer FSG. The love and support from my company and coworkers is amazing.

Leslie will be keeping everyone up to date as this struggle continues. But I will make an effort to chime in every now and then.

Thank you. Forrest

LESLIE: SEPTEMBER 27, 2017

Last month Forrest was diagnosed with ALS—amyotrophic lateral sclerosis. This diagnosis is the absolute worst-case scenario of any diagnosis he could have. When I asked his nurse about his condition, she had no clue what ALS was. This concerned and upset me. But Forrest, in truest Forrest fashion said, "They know I can't breathe well, they know my speech isn't great, and they know I need help moving around. That's what they're focused on, and that's their job. They don't need to know what ALS is to do their job." So now all they can do is to meet each health issue that will come with this diagnosis with medical attention.

So Forrest was having more difficulty than normal breathing late last week. And after an especially hard breathing episode, he felt like it might be another pulmonary embolism. We went to the ER Monday where they confirmed it. They started him back on blood thinners, and he may go home today. They checked his legs for blood clots, and thankfully, they were clear. He's doing better, but his breathing is still labored if he moves around at all.

His care has been good despite my initial reservations. We'll keep you updated on his status.

Side Note: Since then, I've learned that many medical professionals have no clue what ALS is either. This "big disease with the little name" may not affect a lot of people, but it has a huge impact on the person with the disease and their family and friends.

LESLIE: NOVEMBER 13, 2017

When I can't quite understand what Forrest is saying, I'll just say what I think he said. Like this morning I heard "I slept on a burrito," when he was really saying, "I dropped a pill." The only problem with this is when I tell him what I thought he said, it makes him laugh, and when he laughs, he definitely can't speak. That makes us laugh more!

Also, he tells me I'm not allowed to be funny when he's standing up to transfer to the chair or get in the shower because he needs to concentrate. I tell him I'll try, but I sometimes have no control over how funny I am. 😊 😊

LESLIE: APRIL 29, 2018

Sophie (now 6) and Violette (now 4) have been talking a lot more lately about Forrest's ALS diagnosis and all of the changes he and our family have experienced this year. As you can imagine, these are not always easy conversations.

I have been thinking of a visual way for them to see how much they, and our whole family, are loved and supported—and how far-reaching that love is.

Would you help me?

I would like for them to get postcards from across the United States and around the world, if possible! I'm calling this project "A Wave of Love." Wherever you are now, or wherever you may travel, would you consider sending them a postcard? You can put a simple hello, share a story about your adventures or yourself, or simply write a note of love/encouragement.

Thank you for your continued love and support!!

LESLIE: JUNE 1, 2018

This morning was not my best as a mom and caregiver. In all fairness to me, *they all started it*. After being "gritchy" and resistant all morning,

Sophie barely had enough time for breakfast and was late to her Last Day of School. When I came back and was grumping around while I helped Forrest get ready for the day, he pointed to my shirt with a smile on his face. It said, "Nevertheless, She Persisted"—to which I replied, "Today it should say, 'Nevertheless she ended up naked on the floor of 7-Eleven drinking a Slurpee.'" Without skipping a beat, he pointed to his wheelchair, then himself, and said, "I'll take you."

Which of course made me laugh. And broke the grumpy spell. For the most part.

LESLIE, JUNE 26, 2018

Most days Sophie says, "I wish daddy didn't have ALS" and will list the things she misses or wishes he could do. Tonight she said, "I'm glad daddy has ALS. If he didn't, we wouldn't know these 'waves of love' are all around us sending us love and supporting us. And we wouldn't know how important that is."

Somewhere in the middle is where all of our hearts lie—utterly heartbroken for all the things we miss, have lost, and are to come, but filled with immense gratitude for the outpouring of love and care that can only be found in the midst of this kind of heartbreak.

What you have done and are doing with these postcards has had an effect greater than I could have envisioned.

FORREST: AUGUST 29, 2018

One year ago today I was diagnosed with ALS.

Since then I have lost:

The ability to speak.

The ability to walk.

The ability to cough when I need.

The ability to breathe easily.

The ability to dress or shower myself.

My job/career.

The ability to operate a computer or phone.

My independence. I am totally dependent on Leslie and others.

And numerous other things I took for granted.

Every day is more physically taxing than the day before.

I have gained:

A greater understanding of the broken healthcare insurance system.

Precious time with my daughters and wife.

A deeper understanding of the love of my wife.

The grace of others and their generosity.

Wrestling PPV nights with family and friends.

Poker nights with the men of the church.

All that said, I am the same blessed happy person as before. My body is breaking daily. But my awareness of the love in this world continues to amaze me.

Thank you for being my friends. I have avoided Facebook for most of this year. I don't have a reason for it, but I plan on checking in more often.

LESLIE: JANUARY 23, 2019

I had the realization today that it's been almost two years since we made love. I just can't even believe that. I was forty-three years old the last time. I'm grateful that he is still "functional," and we are able to engage in other ways that are pleasing to both of us, but it's still a weird reality that we haven't had intercourse. I'm also grateful that the last time was a *really* good memory to go out on. 😊

LESLIE: MAY 24, 2019

My husband and I have twenty-four hours without our children. We were supposed to do this in March for our anniversary, but one of our kids got sick, so we are celebrating today instead.

In the past, we would have spent this time celebrating: eating good food, talking, laughing, and having creative and fun sex in random places (this is an unplanned double entendre that I'm choosing to keep and giggle about).

Fast forward to today. My husband is napping, and I'm in the den eating fruit and cheese. And he didn't just go and lie down. I had to put him on a sling and transfer him to his sleeping chair, put on a bipap, adjust his shirt, and fix a crease behind his head. And because his legs are so swollen from edema, I had to lift each heavy leg into a compression sleeve that goes from his toes to his hips. Then start the pumps. I'm sitting eating and watching a movie.

That is until I have to get up in fifty-nine minutes and adjust the pumps.

So far, the only sexual part of this day was when I adjusted my husband's balls.

I am one of the lucky ones though. I know this, and I do not take it for granted. I was lucky before ALS, and I'm grateful to still be lucky. He will wake up today. We will have a great evening watching a movie we've been waiting to watch together. And we will still laugh. And I will still be grateful to celebrate another anniversary with him. But I miss his voice. I miss the ease we used to have. And I miss random sex and long lingering touches. Foreplay, innuendo, and anticipation. Although if I'm being completely honest, I really miss before-work quick missionary sex where everyone leaves happy and ready for the day, the most.

LESLIE: SEPTEMBER 19, 2019

I intended to share this beautiful quote I came across this morning and tag Forrest in it, but an unintentional profession of my love fell out of me. Just wanted to give you the heads up.

"Marry your best friend. I do not say that lightly. Really, truly find the strongest, happiest friendship in the person you fall in love with. Someone who speaks highly of you. Someone you can laugh with. The kind of laughs that make your belly ache and your nose snort. The embarrassing, earnest, healing kind of laughs. Wit is important. Life is too short not to love someone who lets you be a fool with them. Make sure they are somebody who lets you cry, too. Despair will come. Find someone that you want to be there with you through those times. Most importantly, marry the one who makes passion, love, and madness combine and course through you. A love that will never dilute—even when the waters get deep and dark." - N'Tima

Forrest, you tread deep waters so beautifully. You make me want to be a better wife, mom, caregiver, friend, and human every single day. You make me laugh every single day. And there is no one in the world I would rather be irritated with, or roll my eyes at, almost every single day. ☺

ALS has taken so fucking much from us, but it has only made my love, commitment, and admiration for you grow stronger. You are an incredible person to do life with. Thank you for being such a tender, calm, compassionate, and thoughtful husband.

LESLIE: JANUARY 29, 2020

For some reason, today has been a day of measuring time and losses because of ALS.

It's been two years since I went to bed on my own schedule. It's been over two years since I've spent a night away from my house. It's almost been two years since I've been to my family's ranch—four years since Forrest was there. It's been three years since Forrest and I ate out together at a restaurant.

It just makes me so sad today. Forrest and I loved to take trips or even just stay in town at a local hotel. Date nights to a restaurant were regular occurrences before and after our kiddos. Our family ranch has been a place of respite my whole life and a place Forrest and I loved to go and take the girls.

The last times I did these things, I was aware of the future we were facing, and I was grateful to have those times; I just didn't realize it would be my last time. At least for a while, this is a reality which is a whole different sadness.

There is nothing to be said to make it better. I'm just going to grieve it today. I'm okay. I'm just feeling all the feelings. And even today, good things happened. We laughed, and we all ate cookies the girls and I made together. It's just that today the sadness felt bigger than all those things. Tomorrow is a new day. Hopefully it will feel different, but it's really okay if it doesn't.

I want to add that these are my feelings and realities associated with ALS. As someone in my support group said, ALS is a family disease. It affects all of us. Nothing I say lessens or takes away from how this disease impacts Forrest. I just needed to write about how it's affecting me today.

I want to tell you that my follow up to this Facebook post was that I told Forrest that he is an anchor, but not in the way he might think. He's an anchor in the way that he provides stability, grounds us, and is our center. *ALS* ties us down and binds us up in negative ways. Never *him*.

LESLIE: MAY 2, 2020

Early yesterday morning, my dad, Lt. Col. Edwin Bright, took his last breaths with Sheila (my stepmom*) by his side. She said it was so peaceful. We knew my dad's time left was short and said our goodbyes to him the day before. My daughters and I were able to be with him after he died and before he was taken to the funeral home. His wishes were to be cremated with no viewing. We will have a memorial service when it's safer for large groups to gather.

I'm so sad he's gone. For most of his life, he was physically a beast of a man. 6'4" and big; in fact, most everyone called him Big Ed. But he was a gentle giant. He never yelled and was never intimidating, but he could leave you in a puddle with a well-placed "I'm disappointed" or "If this is your very best, I'll say great job! Do you feel like you gave this your all?" (When it was clearly something you hadn't given much thought to). He had three daughters, and although he often told us we were pretty, he just as often told us we were powerful and capable. He gave us tire gauges for Christmas one year and taught us how to check our oil and how to put oil in the car. (We always had old cars, so this was an especially important skill.) He was a friend to everyone he met, and there are so many stories of ways he helped different families. He was the Dallas County Agricultural Extension agent for over thirty years and brought 4-H to many counties over our state. I will miss his wisdom so very much. He loved us fiercely and called to check in on us every day.

This experience has been equally heartbreaking and heartwarming. With Covid now affecting so many, I'm thankful he didn't die alone in a hospital. And I'm glad we had some time where he could speak and respond. My girls got to see the gentle, natural progression of a body stopping its work. My oldest daughter observed that "being really sick is hard on your body and makes you very tired."

I couldn't help but think about my PALS, Forrest. I hope and pray when it's his time, it will be peaceful. This experience also prompted me to get him to answer some questions about what he wants to happen after he's gone. I've asked him before, but he hasn't gotten around to answering. I told him I didn't want the burden of not knowing, and he understood that and gave me the responses I needed. I made the calls and researched funeral homes for my dad, and as heartbreaking as it was, it felt empowering to now have the information I need for when

I must do this for Forrest.

But because ALS is ALS, I don't have time to just sit with my own thoughts and grieve. The needs do not go away just because I'm sad or tired. And that makes me feel sad/mad/tired/resentful/grateful. I say grateful because life goes on whether we are ready for it to or not. Having something productive to do helps me not fall too deep in despair. It reminds me that I have a purpose and direction right now—even if it isn't the purpose/direction of my choosing.

I have a legitimate fear that when this is all over, I will never do anything for someone else again. I'm so tired of having to push through to meet the needs of my husband and daughters. And I don't even want to be taken care of; I just want to take care of myself. Eat what I want to eat when I want to eat it, sleep when I want to sleep, and wake up when I want to wake up. But then I feel gut-wrenchingly sad when I realize what would have to happen for me to get my "wish." Fuck ALS and death and the complexity of life. I'm broken, but also happy and okay. It's such a weird place to be.

I'll leave you on a joyful note. This morning my children brought me breakfast in bed and wrote me this incredibly sweet note: "Surprise! We want you to know we appreciate you so much. Here's a little something to recharge you." Life goes on. Love goes on. 💗

*Fun fact: My stepmom is also my aunt. My mom died when I was fourteen, and my dad and my mom's sister got married three years later. So, my dad was also my uncle, and I am technically my own cousin.

LESLIE: JULY 4, 2020

I have an Apple Watch and it has activity goals. I don't even know what they are; they just came set up on the watch, and I've never changed them. I have achieved activity goals doing the following:

Going to the bathroom

Helping Forrest clear his nose

Eating fried chicken

Itching/adjusting Forrest's delicate region

How are you meeting/exceeding your goals? I'm crushing it over here!

LESLIE: SEPTEMBER 1, 2020

The other day Forrest needed help with something. He was pointing in a way that I knew he needed something that was at waist level or lower. Very often I have to ask a series of questions to get to what the need is. Here was my side of the charades (some of this will be TMI, but that has never stopped me from sharing before):

Water?

Remote?

Shirt?

Catheter?

Adjust your chair?

Legs?

Did something fall?

Balls? Is it your balls?

(It was not, in fact, his balls. That time.)

After the fact, I realized Sophie was in the room next to us and was unmuted talking to her teacher. I'm not sure they could hear anything, but all I could think about is this teacher hearing a one-sided conversation with me hollering out these random questions including, "Balls? Is it your balls?!" 😳 😂 😵‍💫

LESLIE: OCTOBER 16, 2020

Goodnight

This simple word had me sobbing last night.

I had tucked Forrest in and said goodnight, when he "said" it back. For the last almost three years, Forrest has used a text-to-speak app on his phone. Bedtime was a hard time for him to text anything because of his being tired, having poor muscle control/coordination, and being in a laid-back position. So, the simple act of saying goodnight became too difficult. For a long time, he would tap his heart to say "I love you," but this has also become more difficult as he has lost his arm movements. About six months ago he stopped being able to text from his phone. He could still use the app with a mouse through his computer but with great difficulty. These changes caused other significant challenges—more than just not hearing him say goodnight. It meant he no longer had the means to easily get my attention or wake me up if he needed help or adjusting during the night. That is a scary and unsettling feeling for both of us, and it caused many sleepless nights.

On Wednesday, we hired someone to help set up and calibrate his Eyegaze machine. This not only means that Forrest can say goodnight back, but now he can also read the news or listen to a book if he's having a sleepless night, and he can alert me if he needs help. Ninety percent of my communication with Forrest these last six months has been me asking a series of questions/options that could be answered with a subtle hand movement, a slight move of his head, or a directional gaze.

Using an Eyegaze is not easy and can be tiring for him, but he has taken to it well, and as you will see, we are all glad to have his "voice" back.

This disease is brutal and unrelenting. It robs us of all the ways we typically communicate and connect. We have adapted well in many ways but having some opportunities for connection and communication back makes me realize how much has been lost, so I appreciate it all the more.

LESLIE: APRIL 19, 2021

I started this letter to myself in early December 2020, right before the anniversary of when the girls came to us on December 11, 2013. I finished writing it tonight. I'm sharing it because I want to share it with y'all and for it to serve as a reminder to myself in the years to come.

Dear Leslie from 2013,

You are right where you are supposed to be, and the path you are about to take will bring you joy, peace, contentment, and connection—the likes of which you have never seen. You will soon meet two girls who will find room in your heart you hadn't known had been waiting for them. Your connection will be instant, and you will feel like you have always known them. Parenthood won't be easy, but it will be worth it. And you will watch them sleep at night after a hard day and your heart will be softened and you will remember the good stuff

53

and make plans to work through the hard stuff. I want to tell you that you may be surprised to know that you also have room waiting for the girls' first family, too. You will love them. Not just because they're your kiddos first family, but because you genuinely love and care for them as your own extended family.

Leslie, I want to tell you that in the next few years, your love for Forrest will grow deeper and more meaningful than you could have ever hoped for. First, you will see him become a father, a role he wears well. Over time, you will learn ways to communicate that you never could have imagined. You will be partners in the truest sense of the word, relying on and drawing strength from each other every day. And you will find joy and make each other laugh. Every. Single. Day. Even on the bad ones.

Leslie, you will also know grief and loss the likes of which you have never seen before. I know that's hard to believe, as you have already known such tremendous loss, but it is true. There is no way to sugarcoat this, so I'm just going to say it. Take some deep breaths, okay?

Leslie, Forrest is going to get really sick. Not cancer sick. There are no treatments for what he gets. He will be diagnosed with ALS. I know you already know what a horrific disease that is, and I'm sorry to say that in 2021, there have still been no advancements toward a cure or significant treatments. It will be bad in all the ways you imagine and in all the ways you can't imagine. You will watch in wonder, horror, and humility as he experiences so many lasts.

So. Many. Lasts.

You will be more prepared for some of the lasts, but it will be the smaller lasts that will break you the most. The last time he puts on his own shoes, the last time he goes to work, the last time he drives a car, the last time he goes to the grocery store. The last time he could pick up a pen and write "I love you" or sign his name. The last time you talked without even realizing what a privilege it was to just talk without effort, without charades, without an electronic device. The last time he was able to pucker his lips for a kiss, the last time he was able to pick up the girls, and the last time he was able to extend his arms and wrap them around us for a hug.

You cannot even list the number of lasts.

Some days you will try, but you will also learn that dwelling on what was won't bring it back or make it better. And you know the day will come that you will witness his last breath. You won't be able to stop that.

No one has ever survived or recovered from ALS.

As parents, we watch with wonder as our children reach each new milestone in their development. There is no word for when someone loses the skills and abilities they grew into and developed. But it is still a privilege to be able to stand alongside someone as those things fade or are lost. This life will be exhausting and overwhelming in all the ways a mind, body, and soul can be.

Why am I telling you all of these oppressive realities? Because you need to know that even in the midst of this, there is normalcy, contentment, and even joy. You will gripe at Forrest because even with ALS, he's still your husband and makes you roll your eyes. Your marriage will be stronger and your admiration for Forrest will increase almost daily. His determination to find a way will push you to do things you didn't think you were capable of doing. You will be a good caregiver. It will not be easy. At all. But you and Forrest will approach everything with humor and honesty, and those two things will get you far.

You really will be okay. I know you won't believe this is possible. But it is true. And it is true because you and Forrest will choose this every day. You choose joy and gratitude over cynicism and anger. And it is true because your friends, family, and even strangers show up in ways you didn't know you needed and weren't sure if you were deserving. You will walk this tightrope unsure if you will fall or stay upright but know that your safety net is there either way. And you will feel God in these moments, too. You will often feel a peace that passes understanding. You will see that grief and joy, loss and acceptance, fear and peace seem to walk hand in hand. You are right where you are supposed to be, and you will be okay.

Love,

Leslie from 2021

LESLIE: MAY 13, 2021

Forrest: I don't know what position to sleep in tonight. Any ideas?

Me: Doggie? Or should we just go with good ol' missionary?

Dudes, nights are still rough around here, and not in the good way. 😩 😂 Last night we basically did not sleep at all. Today his primary nurse practitioner came to check him out, and his eardrum had ruptured. She prescribed him a pain medication that we hoped would help. Tonight, he asked the above question to determine which sleeping position we should start the night out in—and of course I had to take it to the next level. We tried having him mostly upright but slightly reclined. Unfortunately, the combination of lying back at all and wearing his bipap makes his ear hurt horribly. So, we had to get him back up, and now he's sitting up in his wheelchair at his desk hoping to nap a little off and on.

I'm going to head to bed to try to sleep for a few hours. It's hard for me to unwind when I'm this exhausted and on edge, but I'm hoping to get some rest.

All of this is to say, "position" talk just isn't as fun now as it once was. (It's okay to laugh even if you feel sorry for us. We feel sorry for us and still laugh at ourselves. 😄)

LESLIE: FEBRUARY 14, 2022

Today I told Forrest that since it was Valentine's Day, I wanted him to just lie back and let me do everything for him. Just sit back and relax, and his every wish was my command.

And then we laughed and laughed and laughed. 😄

I did tell him that today I would do all those things that I normally do, but with good humor, and I will not be bitchy. Until 6:00 p.m....
then I can't help what happens or how I act.

Thank goodness we both still have a sense of humor.

LESLIE: APRIL 16, 2022

When someone is dying and there is a known or anticipated "expiration" date, you drop everything and sit in that moment. You are encouraged to put everything else aside (school, activities, cleaning, etc) and just be by the side of your loved one in those final days.

When someone has a terminal illness like ALS, you know from the start how that story will end, but what you don't know is if it's a short story or a chapter book. A sprint or a marathon. If/when you make it through the first year or so you start to think to yourself, "Well, death didn't come this year. What now? I guess I better figure out how to live with this." What does that even look like? How do you acknowledge the reality and impending weight of death/loss and still "live?" And, hopefully, live well, not just survive. For us it meant facing the reality but weaving normalcy into the daily anticipation of knowing someone is going to die sooner rather than later. You have to try to keep on keeping on.

As I think about Forrest's surgery on Thursday, I can't help but consider the worst case scenario. I have been subconsciously counting down the days and wondering if I'm soaking up and making the most of these days that may be "the lasts." At the same time, I'm just trying to do all the daily things that have to be done. And if this surgery is just the "next chapter" in the ALS journey, and not "the last", then I need to conserve energy and take care of myself so I'm ready for the next set of challenges that will inevitably come. I'm in for the long haul and need to be ready for that too. I find myself going between wanting to just sit next to him and be with him continuously and a desire to run off and be completely alone with no thoughts or needs but my own.

It's all really beautiful and brutal. I have fallen in love with Forrest more each day that I've been his caregiver. We are together almost 24/7 now. He is my day and night. My mind does not have a space anymore where wondering about him and his needs does not exist. That's the reality of caregiving for someone who requires this level of care. It's not healthy, but it's the reality. And I recognize that I am fortunate to deeply love and enjoy the person I'm taking care of—that's not the case for everyone.

The depth of that love and the weight of caregiving will mean that when death comes, my loss will feel so much greater and my relief equally great. I will lose my purpose and will be freed to find a new purpose at the same time. Grieving minds sometimes have a hard time reconciling those two realities, and I wonder how I will manage all of that, if I can handle it all. Those are realities for another day, but they creep into my wonderings, and I can't help but feel the seesaw of freedom and despair looming.

Today everyone needs to be dressed, fed, and tended to. Cheese grits need to be made for Easter, and the house needs to be picked up. The "normalcy" is both a welcome distraction and a weight. But all these thoughts and feelings will still be there. Swimming in the sea of this McKinney/ALS life.

This is why it's hard to answer the questions of "How are you doing?" Or "How are things going?"

This is what anticipatory grief looks and feels like to me.

FORREST: April 18, 2022

To: Leslie McKinney

Subject: Surgery to Get My Feeding Tube and My Dying Wishes

"Don't forget what happened to the man who suddenly got everything he wanted. He lived happily ever after." —Willy Wonka

I think everything will go fine with the surgery on Thursday. But if it doesn't, I need you to know that I think it's necessary and past the time when I needed it. I am confident in my team and our preparation for this. I'm aware of all the risks.

I want you to know that I don't know how I will be when I come back home from the hospital. I have been reading about going under anesthesia in my condition and the possible outcomes. I could not be the same as I am now. But we will handle it however I am when I get home. I have every confidence in our ability to adapt.

If the worse happens and I die, I am prepared for that outcome. There are several things that I want to share with you about my wishes when I die, whether in the surgery or after many more years.

First, I am happy with my life, and like the quote above, I have everything I could wish for to have lived happily ever after. I know that I have been an anchor that has kept you from going anywhere for the last few years and wish you and the girls would go and do everything and enjoy yourselves. I wish you would plan on going to Disney World and experience that with the girls. And while there I hope that you will take them to the ocean. Also, take them to the ranch as much as possible. That is a special place to me.

If you fall in love with someone else, I only wish you happiness. I know that they will be a good parent to our girls if you are in love with them. I trust you and your judgment about everything. You have an awful big heart and rocking body and have a lot to offer someone. The person will be so lucky to be in your life. I wish you all the happiness in the world in the next phase of your and the girls' lives.

That is all I can hope for.

I love you and Sophie and Violette forever-ever.

LESLIE: MAY 26, 2022

Yesterday was a good day. Even though he is in the hospital, Forrest was more his normal self. I squirted a little water and some coffee in

60

his mouth, and he was able to swallow some. He was using his bi-pap, but his oxygen level was 100% without oxygen or anything. He was able to use his Eyegaze and communicate. Overall, he just seemed more his normal self.

Around nine o'clock I was heading out to go home to sleep, and he asked me to kiss him and told me he loved me and to sleep well. Around two o'clock in the morning I got a call that his blood pressure tanked, and they had to give him meds to get it up. He was stable at the time, and he didn't want me to come back up there. About thirty minutes later I got a call that he crashed, blood pressure dropped more, he vomited a small amount of blood, and with the assumption that his ulcer was bleeding again, they intubated him to protect his airway.

By the time I got up there they had given him four units of blood and were prepping him for a test to check the bleeding. They were able to stabilize him again, and we waited for GI to consult this afternoon. They did another EGD and were pleased to see that while he was having some intermittent bleeding, the ulcers are healing. They also did a colonoscopy and discovered that his bowels were severely impacted. The doctor cleaned a good bit of "it" out and has ordered "rocket fuel" to blast out the rest. While the procedures weren't lengthy, the doctor said Forrest needed to rest and just take it easy because his body is processing and adjusting to a lot, so he is still sedated and intubated.

I was thinking today about these hurdles. Under normal circumstances you would get through each of these with the thought of "Oh good, after this we can recover and move on." But that is just not the ALS life.

This doctor is saying that Forrest will need to be on a bowel regimen where he is having bowel movements twice a day. He is 6'2", 275 pounds, and quadriplegic. What the hell does twice a day pooping look like?! All I know is that there is no one who can tell me what to do, and I'll just end up figuring it out—most likely with the infinite wisdom of my ALS support group. And if we get through this hurdle, what and when will be the next? This one was terrifying. He was throwing up blood profusely. I've now gone four days without seeing our children in person during their last week of school and after feeling the shock from the murders of the elementary school children here in Texas. It's hard not to feel overwhelmed with the conflicting feelings of wanting him to recover and the thoughts of "but then what?"

You ALS caregivers will appreciate what I did today. I didn't get up to silence alarms, I didn't get up to suction, I didn't get up to adjust or clean him up. I was a worried wife, and I let the hospital nurses do their jobs. I'm headed home now (at seven-thirty at night) to enjoy my dinner and hopefully a long, good night of sleep. I do not feel guilty. Forrest would have encouraged me to do this, and I have also reminded myself that this is the normal and natural way of things. It is not normal to be the sole caregiver for another human 24/7.

One last note, to end in good humor. I cannot wait for Forrest to wake up so I can tell him that we now have confirmation that he's full of shit.

LESLIE: JUNE 16, 2022

Catching up. It's been an eventful 48 hours.

Forrest is still in the hospital and continuing to recover from his GI bleed. His hemoglobin numbers are very slowly starting to become steady. We've been waiting for that. Tomorrow they will remove his old PICC line and put in a tunneled line because there is a blood clot near it. Because of his bleeding, he can no longer be on blood thinners, which is a little unnerving for someone with a history of pulmonary embolism. At this point we are just having to weigh risks versus rewards.

Now for me.

For a few days I was having cramping in my hands and legs. Then a few days ago, I started experiencing numbness and tingling in my extremities. I was concerned and decided to go ahead and walk down to the emergency room. They determined that my calcium was critically low. They told me that I would need to be admitted because the dosage of calcium I needed has to be monitored when they're giving it because it can cause heart problems. Thankfully, I was given a couple of doses over the last day and a half without incident. I was released from the hospital this afternoon, then went upstairs to be with Forrest for a while.

I left about four o'clock to head out to see the girls who were not aware that I had been sick since they were staying with my sister Lisa and her family. This afternoon I started feeling poorly and took my temperature. It was 99.6. Then I decided to take a Covid test. It was positive.

Ugh. I just don't even know what to do or say about all of this. I'm glad that for the most part I haven't been with Forrest for the last forty-eight hours, but being in the hospital is very difficult for him. I'm thankful that Sheila was with him last night, and Pat has been with him today.

LESLIE: OCTOBER 21, 2022

(five days before Forrest died)

After almost five months of hell, I feel like I finally have my husband back. I'm posting this because I feel relieved and also in case it's helpful to someone else.

First things first. Forrest is fifty-one years old, bulbar onset over six years ago, diagnosed five years ago. He has not spoken verbally in five years, hasn't walked in four years, and has been almost completely quadriplegic for the last year. He still breathes on his own during the day and uses a bipap at night.

After surgery in April and then two hospitalizations in May and June, Forrest ended up in a great deal of pain. Prior to April of this year, he rarely had any kind of pain, and if he took Tylenol, Advil, or Aleve, it relieved it.

All of that changed after his hospitalizations. He had several injuries because of the poor care he received. When he came home from each hospital stay, he was a mess. Agitated to the point that his breathing was erratic, he would have full body spasms.

His palliative care doctor started him on Tramadol and Ativan. Things continued to get worse. He couldn't communicate or use his Eyegaze because he was either in too much pain or agitated. He was set off by any minor discomfort. And this was happening all day and all night, to the point that he was crying out in the night so loud our kids were scared. This is not and has not been anything like my husband before. I was at my wits end and was the nastiest I've been since this ALS journey started. I couldn't handle the relentless, torturous nature of where we were.

The palliative care doctor upped and changed meds to adjust to his increasing needs. They seemed to work for a day or two; then we were back to the drawing board.

He ended up taking the following medications: Tramadol, Ativan. Valium, Depakote, hydrocodone, Wellbutrin, and baclofen.

Through a series of irritating issues with insurance, he ended up not having his Valium for a couple of days, and he seemed better on those days. I mentioned it to him, and he agreed he felt better. Ativan and Valium are in the same family of drugs, so I wondered if he would feel better without Valium, would he feel better without Ativan? He also wanted to see.

I am not exaggerating when I say that the last two weeks have been life-changing. I went from begging for death daily (just to be able to get a break or relief!) to being so grateful for this time with my husband. He stopped the Ativan, Valium, and Wellbutrin completely. He is taking the others in small doses which seems to be giving him the balance he needs. He is so much happier. He can use his Eyegaze so much easier. He's chatting and charming which is how he was before April of this year. He is still in some pain and needs to be adjusted, but he isn't demanding and agitated. He has been so grateful, supportive, and encouraging to me.

Don't get me wrong, he still has ALS, and all the needs that go along with where he is right now. But he found his charm and humor again, and I'm so incredibly happy to see him again. I have missed him, and I didn't think I was going to have more time with that part of him.

I'm sharing this as a cautionary tale. Sometimes the remedy is or becomes the problem. Don't be afraid to trust your gut and work with your team to make sure your PALS is getting what works best for them.

LESLIE: DECEMBER 31, 2022

Dear 2022,

You were, by far, my most difficult year. I leave you worse off than I found you and leery of the work and recovery yet to come. I have cried more and had my mental, physical, and emotional metal pushed, stretched, and tested more than I thought possible. I am bent, frayed, and jagged as a result.

Despite all of this, I will miss you dearly. You hold the last precious moments with my love. There will be no Forrest in 2023. No New Year's kiss and no new memories to be made.

You will pass the torch to 2023 in a matter of a few hours, unscathed by the havoc left behind. Because there was no malice or unkept promise. You are merely a marker for what was and what is yet to be. So, I would like to say this. I am grateful to have seen your beginning and your end. I will treasure the many moments of love, joy, and laughter this year captured. And with immense gratitude, I keep with me the new memories made with Sophie and Violette, old friendships deepened, and new friendships formed.

I leave with you so much heartache, the challenges of 24/7 caregiving, the plaguing fear and worry of anticipatory grief, and the monster that is ALS. The new year will come whether I'm ready to say goodbye to you or not. I plan to welcome her with open arms. Ready to meet the next chapter. Hopeful that stability, healing, and joy will be threads that connect the next 365 days. Aware that challenges will come and with the knowledge that I'll be capable of meeting them with grace, love, and resilience through the support and encouragement of the best family and friends.

And through the lasting legacy of the beautiful life of Forrest McKinney.

REFRAMING MY LIMITED LIFE

KERRIN RUMMEL

I said I would…

I need to get…

These days I have a hard time remembering anything even long enough to write it down.

One thing I do still remember is the date my life changed.

It was the morning of Thursday, October 7, 2010. I woke up with a tickle in my throat that told me I was coming down with a cold. Although I was very busy at work as a senior mechanical engineer for Raytheon, I decided to take off Friday and clear my weekend plans in hope of feeling back up to full speed on Monday. It was not even in my mind that I might never get back to full speed again. That weekend, weakness, fatigue, flu symptoms, and brain fog plagued me.

The following week, I started what seemed to be a never-ending round of visiting doctors, only to be told they could find nothing wrong with me.

After a quick visit with an urgent care doctor and diagnosis of an asymptomatic bladder infection, a round of antibiotics cured the bladder infection but not any of the symptoms that were causing my discomfort.

My first specialist visit was to my gynecologist, "my favorite doctor." After determining there was nothing wrong with me in his area of medicine, he looked at me very sadly and told me that I would need many doctor visits and tests to determine for sure, but his expectation was that I would ultimately be diagnosed with Chronic Fatigue Syndrome (CFS, now currently referred to as ME/CFS or myalgic encephalomyelitis/chronic fatigue syndrome), a life-changing chronic illness with no approved treatments. As disappointing and frustrating as that was, I was very fortunate to have been diagnosed early in my illness. It is much more typical for patients to go for months or even years without a diagnosis because it is still a diagnosis of exclusion.

Since there are no established tests or physiological markers to positively diagnose ME/CFS, doctors have to test for and rule out everything else it could be. It turns out that there are many illnesses that share symptoms with ME/CFS. Although there is a great deal of research showing the numerous physiological changes that come with this illness, many doctors believe and are still being taught that this is a psychosomatic illness with no basis in biology. With the 2020 Covid pandemic infecting millions of people, we are now seeing an unfortunate, large population experiencing symptoms in common with ME/CFS. Some of these people are being diagnosed with long Covid. I am hopeful that in the near future all the research on ME/CFS diagnosis and management will be used to help the long Covid patients and that the extensive research now being conducted on long Covid will ultimately prove valuable to the ME/CFS patients.

Before my illness, my life was probably typical of working mothers of teenagers. I worked hard to find the balance between my job and my family. Everything else—household chores, cooking, socialization—was relegated to the corners of my life. I stuffed them in wherever I could find an unoccupied space on my schedule or multitasked with other activities.

I loved my job. It gave me the perfect combination of intellectual stimulation, socialization, and leadership. I would often say it was lucky that I got paid for it, since I would have done it for free. I worked with some of the most advanced technology in the world. I did my own research to develop technologies needed for future systems, resulting in several patents. I had the privilege of providing technical supervision for some of the most brilliant young engineers I had ever met. I also did scheduling, budgeting, and proposal writing for a variety of contracts.

Several of my mentors were anxious for me to pursue a promotion. But I was very open about the fact that I was happy with my work/life balance and would not work towards or accept a new position that required more time away from my family. I fully anticipated looking for new opportunities after Jason, my youngest child, left for college. At the time I became ill, we were just a few weeks away from a major work deadline, so things were stressful but positive. We were working hard and making great progress. I didn't have time to be sick!

I also tried to stay as involved in my children's and husband's lives as possible. I had recently returned from dropping off my daughter Shannon for her freshman year at college. Since her university was close to my parents' home in Southern California, I spent a wonderful few days with them during and after the move in. My son Jason was a sophomore in high school; he was learning to drive and starting to think about what his future might hold. My husband Doug was a science teacher and robotics coach at the height of robotics season. He also didn't have time for me to be sick.

In addition to my crushing fatigue and continuing flu-like symptoms, I also developed severe brain fog and memory issues. Before my illness, I never kept a written to-do list. I could remember and prioritize necessary tasks for multiple projects. After I became ill, I couldn't remember tasks and had to maintain a written list. Often, I would review that to-do list and find it filled with incomplete sentences; I would commit to completing a task, but I couldn't remember it long enough to write it down.

After a couple of weeks of trying to keep up with my life, I decided I could no longer continue my work at Raytheon and took a short-term leave of absence in order to concentrate on improving my health. This is when the great doctor hunt began. Ultimately, I consulted at least a dozen doctors who ordered about 400 unique tests of bodily fluids in an attempt to find something wrong with me that could be treated. With each test, my husband and I were relieved that I tested negative for these often very horrible diseases and frustrated that there was nothing that would make me better.

While we tried to allow Shannon to focus on her college experience and not concern her with the day-to-day stress of all of this, our children are exceedingly close, so they talked to each other. I remember once Jason called Shannon at college to tell her, "Good news—Mom doesn't have cancer."

I had thought we were doing a good job of communicating with our children, but I was unaware that Jason was concerned about cancer. His call to Shannon worried her more because we had not been keeping her in the loop.

When I had used up my sick leave from work, I applied for disability status. It was denied because I did not have a diagnosable illness. Because I loved my job and was dedicated to the projects I was involved in, I pushed myself to work half time as often as I could. My days consisted of four hours of focused, productive work before I had to leave the office. I would grab the quickest lunch I could find, then collapse in bed for a four-hour nap. Then it took me another hour or two to be able to move to the living room and plop into my recliner. I couldn't do anything but eat and be present with Doug and Jason until the next day when I started the cycle all over again.

I would follow this pattern for a few months until I couldn't even walk into work on a Monday morning. Then I would take a leave of absence until I felt strong enough to go to work again.

In between doctor visits and tests, I was researching to find out as much as I could about ME/CFS and any treatments for it that were being tested. I came across work being done at University of the Pacific in Stockton, California, where they used a two-day exercise test to demonstrate ME/CFS patients' abnormal reactions to exercise. As a scientist, this study intrigued me. I wondered if I could use it to get my disability status approved; it had already been denied several times. I wasn't really interested in getting full-time disability because I loved my job and wanted to keep working, but I knew I needed a disability status.

I applied to get tested, and they connected me with a disability lawyer and a ME/CFS specialist doctor, all in California. Ultimately, I went through the two-day exercise test in addition to some specialized cognitive testing. These tests determined that I was as disabled as someone with serious heart disease, and they also revealed that I had significant cognitive impairment.

The specialist told me I should never work again. That was the end of my beloved career.

It was very difficult to retire at the early age of fifty when I was not at all ready to retire. Thankfully, the data from these tests and a very persuasive lawyer allowed me to get disability coverage through the company insurance and Social Security, softening the financial blow a little.

Much of this first phase of my illness was focused on learning to live with it. Many times, when I was busy at work and felt good, I would work a full day instead of half a day. It felt good at the time to get tasks checked off of my to-do list. But the next day I couldn't drag myself to work. This is the push-and-crash cycle typical of ME/CFS patients because we don't feel tired until after we have done far too much. One of the hardest lessons to learn about living with this illness is recognizing when you have hit your limit—and stopping *then*. It is made harder by the fact that any activity short of lying down is fatiguing—even a cognitive activity like reading.

When people with ME/CFS overdo cognitive or physical activity, they are likely to experience post exertional malaise (PEM). Everyone experiences their own version of PEM, but for me it often included a return to debilitating fatigue, dizziness sometimes even while sitting, and flu-like symptoms. For this reason, the most important lesson I had to learn was pacing. Through experience, I learned to estimate what activity combinations were likely to trigger my PEM and to avoid them wherever possible. I also regularly made decisions to join in on activities knowing I was risking PEM because the activities were that important to me. Attending my daughter's wedding, hosting Thanksgiving, joining social gatherings, traveling, and even writing this book chapter were among the activities I engaged in knowing the risk to my health.

Ultimately, after all the various doctors had run out of tests, I ended up with two specialists who dealt with my most pressing symptoms. My ME/CFS specialist in California was deeply involved in the research that was happening in the area as well as doing some of his own. He always had new tests for me to take and new treatments to try. None of these were expected to cure me, but in small ways, they improved my quality of life.

I also found a local cardiologist who specializes in orthostatic intolerance which initially was one of my biggest problems. My body had forgotten how to regulate my circulatory system to compensate for my movement into different positions. As a result, I was at risk of fainting anytime I stood up or walked. Between these two doctors, I now have a regimen of seven prescription medications and eleven supplements that combine to keep me stable and functioning at my current minimal level.

For a full two years, I alternated half-time work with extended leaves of absence. This was very frustrating as I missed my work both financially and intellectually. But this change did bring with it some real joys, including being able to appreciate quiet afternoons talking to my teenage son about school, life, and his dreams.

I also was able to spend a summer living with Shannon across the street from the beach as she finished up her final college classes. She was taking three classes in each of the two summer terms. As she toiled away on her schoolwork, I was able to enjoy the cool summer and time at the beach. When we both needed a break, she would push my wheelchair around the weekly market in town, or we would rent a tandem kayak and paddle around the marina next to our apartment and check out the sea lions lounging on the docks. While she was at school, I would rest in our apartment or head out to the beach for some time on the sand. While I love to swim in the ocean, I didn't dare do more than wade in a few inches since I didn't trust I would have the energy to get myself out.

My parents lived about two hours away, but Shannon's compressed school schedule made it difficult to find time to spend together. It happened that her single day off between terms came a few days after my fifty-second birthday. My parents planned to come down and spend the day with us and have a little birthday celebration.

Immediately after our return to the apartment from Shannon's day of finals, I got a call from my dad. He said that my mom had been involved in a fatal car accident. It took me a moment to realize that my mom had died. I found out later that she had been missing since the evening before, but my father had just been informed that the car and my mother's body had been found.

After a quick review of her upcoming classes, Shannon determined that she could access all the materials online. So, while I was driving us up to be with my dad, she emailed all her professors to say she would be doing her schoolwork remotely for the first week of the second summer session. I was able to spend those first two weeks with my dad helping him prepare for the memorial service and all the other duties that are so difficult to do in the wake of a sudden death. After Shannon's summer schoolwork ended, I spent another couple of weeks with my dad before we headed back to Texas. I would never have been able to do all of this had I still been working. As much as I missed my career, I treasured the opportunities I was given.

〜

After I was told that I was neither adequately healthy nor cognitively fit to continue my work at any level, I had to figure out what my future life was going to look like. I had difficulty finding a purpose to living.

I was working with one of the premiere specialists in the country for my illness, hoping for a treatment that would restore my ability to work and do the other activities I loved. But I had to accept the fact that full recovery was unlikely to happen. All the things I had once stuck into the corners of my life—laundry, cooking, cleaning, spending time with friends—became my entire life. All the energy I had stored up each day was spent trying to keep up with household chores. At first, I was unable even to cook a full meal since I could not stand up for any period of time. How could I go from an active and intellectual life to just *sitting* in front of the TV every day? I even had to give up reading books because it was too stressful cognitively.

I found audiobooks from my local library and podcasts that I could listen to. I started crocheting again, a hobby I learned in high school. I had made a few things over the years—although that ended with the still-incomplete baby blanket for my twenty-eight-year-old son. Now that I had time again, I enjoyed making things for my family, their friends, and for a Dallas non-profit called Spreading the Warmth. I made Pokémon creatures for my daughter, now a teacher, to display in her middle-school classroom. Her students enjoyed the sense of discovery when they noticed a new creature on a shelf in the classroom. Slowly, I was finding ways to stay challenged and to feel purpose.

In 2016, we completed a full remodel of our home. This update gave us an opportunity to redesign the kitchen so that I could spend more time there. Over the last several years, working at my seated workstation in the kitchen has become one of my great joys. It is one of the few things I can do to help manage our household and take some of the burden off the other family members. Many days, one of my morning chores is to do the prep work for the evening's dinner. I don't have the energy to make a meal from scratch all at once, but I can make it if I spread the tasks out throughout the day. I often try new recipes because it gives me a sense of adventure. When I was first ill, I focused on learning to bake bread. The yummy bread was a great treat for the entire family and gave me a sense of accomplishment.

My mother had set a wonderful example for me about how to approach life with a chronic illness. She had been diagnosed with multiple sclerosis in her late thirties when I was in high school. She, too, had to give up a job she loved in order to get more rest and manage her illness. Over the following decades, she traveled the world with my father (my brother used her considerable stack of passports as a prop for her eulogy) and kept up an active social and charity calendar. She showed me how important it is to find ways to do what you want to do, even if it is done on a smaller scale, while also treating yourself kindly and giving in to the illness when necessary.

Now I am trying to be that example to my daughter; at twenty-nine years old, Shannon was diagnosed with multiple sclerosis. Between my mother's example and my own, I am hoping to show Shannon that there is a path around her illness to living a fulfilling and joyful life.

After five years as an accomplished middle school science teacher, she switched to teaching in a virtual charter school. This career change allowed her to pursue her lifelong passion for education without the physical burden of standing all day long. Online education is a very different teaching experience, but she has adapted to the new challenges well. Shannon recently married a wonderful man who has been supportive during her initial diagnosis and ongoing treatment. Their lives will be different than what they initially imagined, but they are committed to making their time together adventurous and fulfilling.

I also have found record keeping to be very important. Due to my issues with brain fog, I tried to have a family member at as many doctor appointments as possible. Along with my husband, that has included my parents and my young adult children. Some doctors were uncomfortable with my children being included. Others embraced it and asked my kids about their experience with me during my illness.

Many ME/CFS patients struggle with making their families understand that they are truly ill. I'm lucky since I never had that problem with any close family members; they immediately knew that my abrupt change in behavior had to be the result of something terribly wrong.

On the advice of one of the first doctors I saw after I became ill, I kept copies of all my test reports, visit notes, and procedures. I even have a massive spreadsheet of all my bodily fluid test results. This information is crucial since no single doctor can absorb all of it. There have been times when a doctor would see a pattern in two yearly test results—but I could use the data on my spreadsheet to show it was a random variation, not a disturbing pattern.

Like my parents, one of the passions my husband Doug and I share is traveling, and it was very important for us to find ways to continue to travel, even with my illness. The summer before I became ill, we took a trip to Europe with our extended family to celebrate my daughter's high school graduation and my parents' fiftieth wedding anniversary. We had a fabulous time exploring Venice and the hill towns of Tuscany and Umbria, a trip I would be unable to take now. We spent long, hot days walking up steep hills and stairs. It was beautiful and very special. I'm so glad we had a chance to do it then.

To travel now, we must find places that won't be too hot and are wheelchair accessible. While I was in the process of finding the right medications and pacing to make the most of the energy I had, even short plane flights to see my family were difficult but worth the effort. I learned early on to rest where I could, even if it meant resting on a coat spread out on an airport floor. I need a nap every day. It does not necessarily mean sleeping but just giving my body a rest from the orthostatic stress. I also need to be as close to horizontal as possible or exhaustion will overcome me, and I will not be able to sit up until I have had the rest. This need for rest and self-care causes some scheduling issues in ordinary life but more so while traveling.

In 2019, we decided to attempt longer, more complex trips, including a six-week trip to the British Isles. In 2022, we took a seven-week road trip around the United States which included participating in our daughter's out-of-town wedding. These trips were carefully planned to accommodate my needs. We purchased premium economy seats on the transatlantic flight. The two-seat row configuration allowed me to stretch out over our two seats to get some of the rest from the orthostatic stress. We used a rugged wheelchair that could handle curbs and a variety of terrains. With that wheelchair, we carried all our luggage on the public transportation as well as traversed miles of London streets.

If we couldn't find ways to schedule a return to our home base by midday for my rest period, we found other ways for me to rest. I have rested in the back seat of cars, in a public park in Dublin, and on the grounds of historical sites. Even with all the planning, I need to go into these trips with the assumption that there will be days I just need some extra rest. Starting with this expectation, it doesn't feel like I'm losing as much valuable travel time.

Doug has learned that there are days and outings that he must do alone. He has found this to be pleasant when he has an extra travel partner, like when he spent the day in Cork with his brother who joined us for our Ireland tour. He also will spend a day doing something he enjoys doing that I don't, like fishing at Yellowstone National Park. When just the two of us are traveling, he will often use my nap times for short, scenic walks or to plan our future outings.

It has been very important to me to find the blessings that have come with my illness. It helps to balance the frustration I experience with all the things I can no longer do. Among the blessings are the special times I spend with my children, the extra time I had with my dad following my mother's death, and the extensive travel we have been able to do without the past vacation limits of having a job.

Now that Doug has retired, I'm hopeful I'll be able to get out more. I'm grateful for his availability to help with driving and pushing my wheelchair, as his help allows us to go on walks or to the store—things that I've been unable to do alone. His extra support with the daily household tasks also allows me to expend more of my energy on fun activities like seeing a movie, eating lunch out, or helping Shannon with tasks she can't do alone.

We also are hoping to push the envelope and travel even more extensively in the future. We've always wanted to travel to Australia and New Zealand, but the long plane flights feel very daunting. Since I've managed a flight to Europe, we are working towards extending my flying time by planning a trip to Asia for the coming year.

Shannon recently told me she has learned to not be afraid to ask for help as she navigates through her multiple sclerosis. Unfortunately, though, she did not learn this from my example because I always have been a proudly independent person. This character trait probably is an innate part of my personality, but it surely was reinforced by my many years spent working "in a man's world." Shannon told me she remembers pushing me in my wheelchair when we were out together and that it didn't seem like a burden. So now when she asks her friends or husband to push her in a wheelchair, she tries to remember this and realizes that it probably isn't a burden for them, either.

In the future, I will try to remember this when I know I need help. After thirteen years of dealing with my chronic illness, the most difficult aspect of it is still the loss of my independence.

The exercise physiologist who did my exercise testing is known for saying "housework is exercise." This seemingly simple statement has stuck with me for years and has helped me in many ways. If I walk around the house all day, then that is all the exercise I need. If I have spent most of the day sitting, then I will take a short walk or use my seated exercise machine. Now when doctors ask if I'm exercising regularly, I tell them about my latest daily walking goal, and they are usually satisfied.

Today, I am no longer hoping for a cure or a treatment that will give me my prior health back, but I'm always trying to find something that will *improve* it. I try to keep up with the research being done for my illness, and now for long Covid, always looking for something I can try that might help alleviate my pain.

As I know I'll probably be in this condition for the remainder of my life, I've learned that I should stop thinking that I *can't* do something; rather, I should find a way to reframe the challenge so I *can* do it. I can't read for any extended time, but I can listen to audiobooks and podcasts. I can't do computer work in a straight back chair, but I can work for a short time in my recliner. I'm thankful to be learning that I can be productive and valuable. I can make my life joyful, even in my limited capacity.

When I was first approached about writing my story for this book, I couldn't imagine I would ever have the energy to write it. I began working on it many times, but after just fifteen minutes, I had to put my writing aside. *Would I ever finish it?*

Thankfully, I reframed this challenge and over many months kept writing in small segments of just a few sentences until my story was complete. I hope that through reading it, you'll be inspired to reframe any limiting situation that comes your way and still discover ways to be productive and to find joy.

FINDING MY STEPS FORWARD

JULIA L. WILLIAMS DADE

You were never created to live depressed, defeated, guilty, condemned, ashamed, or unworthy.

–Joel Osteen

Writing about my life brings to mind so many memories from this tragic event that I often find myself in tears. I don't think my tears will ever stop flowing.

When you lose a child to suicide, it is a reality that is not explainable or understandable. *How does one move forward once your beloved child has chosen to leave this earth?*

I had to find a way to move forward.

~~~~~

I was born into a Southern Black American family and was raised by exceptional parents. My father, Robert A. Minus, was born in 1915. He was five years old when The Tulsa Massacre occurred in the area of Oklahoma called the Black Wall Street. His mother's business was destroyed along with almost the entire neighborhood he'd come to call home. In the following years, he saw his stepfather, H.C. Williams, build an addition onto his family's home so that "Miss Hattie" could continue her vocation as a beautician.

In 1939, World War II broke out, and all able-bodied men enlisted or were drafted. Many Black Americans joined the military ranks not only to defend their country but also to receive pay while learning a valuable trade that could possibly help them later in life. My father told stories about flying in an airplane, visiting different cities, and seeing many beautiful sites. He received a Bronze Star for meritorious service in a combat zone. When he returned to the States at the end of the war, he met and married my mother, Suddie Mae, built a house, and started his family.

My dad was a soft-spoken man with the biggest smile. When I think of Bible verses that mention God's loving arms wrapped around us, I think of the times my dad would hold me in his arms. His pet nickname for me was "Skeeta" because he said I was so little that I was no heavier than a mosquito. Both my mom and dad were determined to give their children the best of everything they could. It wasn't until later in my life that I realized how much of a foundation they had given us so that we could live our dreams.

My mother was an intelligent woman who was set to be the valedictorian of her high school class until she was told to stay home and take care of the house while her father and brothers were out working as sharecroppers. But she continued to be passionate about her education and worked hard to pull herself up. My mother also had a deep love for music. We'd often hear her singing some tune while she was washing dishes. She definitely passed on her love for music to each of her seven children.

My siblings and I all learned how to swim and how to play classical music on the piano. My sisters and I took ballet, while my brothers took tap lessons. I found it amazing that my parents searched until they found the "diamond cutters" in the community to help provide a well-rounded education for their children. These people knew how to recognize and work with raw talent. Growing up in a faith-based Black community that was invested in every child was liberating.

I find that the older I get, the more I realize how intelligent my parents were. I was the second of seven children, and I used to give my mom grief because she never worked outside the home. Little did my young mind know that my mom attended college, and it was my dad who dropped out of high school to enlist and fight in World War II.

My parents had decided they didn't want anyone else to raise their children once they'd started their family. Mom knew her kids needed to understand what a good education would do for them, so she made sure that they learned to take advantage of every opportunity for success that she could find. Throughout my life, the life skills that my mom taught me sustained me.

But I still wonder how my parents pulled off shielding me from racism until I was twelve years old. It was in 1968 while we were living in Tulsa, Oklahoma, when we received the news that Dr. Martin Luther King, Jr was assassinated. Amazingly, I had no idea that the United States of America had been experiencing the life-changing events of the Civil Rights Movement.

In early 1973, it was almost my senior year of high school—a year that most teenagers face with excitement and joy. Would they go to college or tech school when they graduated? Could they share a dorm room with one of their good friends?

But I didn't have the privilege of worrying about these life-changing decisions because I had a secret that no one knew. I was pregnant! It was late in my junior year, and my boyfriend was a senior. When he found out I was pregnant, he freaked out and didn't want to have anything else to do with me. I didn't know what I was going to do. Thankfully, after talking with my school counselor and parents, we worked together on the next course of action.

It was my mother who unequivocally showed me her support by telling me, "You work on getting an education, and I'll take care of your child." Her words have come to my mind over the years and have helped me understand the tenacity it takes to lovingly guide your children in the best direction you can, regardless of the circumstances and many sacrifices it takes to get them there.

I finished my high school education after my son Christopher was born, and I started community college in the fall. As I struggled through my first year of college, it was disheartening to realize that managing my home life, college life, and working part-time were making me feel like I was barely treading water. It wasn't until my high school counselor who'd kept in touch with me suggested that I go out of town to college that I started to realize how big of a task I was biting off by being a working student and the parent of a newborn. I had to enroll somewhere, apply for financial aid, and decide on a major. Once again, my parents supported me and encouraged me to live on campus at Oklahoma State University and experience all that college life offered. In turn, they took care of Christopher.

It was touch and go with my studies for that second year of college at OSU, especially since I didn't know anyone. My roommate was never around, but there was a college organization called "The African American Society" that had a rather large office where students could drop by between classes and meet other like-minded students. Throughout my time at OSU, it was at that office that I made life-long friends, found support and acceptance, and began to chart my course of study.

During my third year in college, I found myself at the campus library talking to a bright young man named Herman. Not too long after our first few encounters, we started to date. We'd attended a few on-campus activities together, but it wasn't until he asked me why I didn't study more that our relationship changed. I felt my grades were "so-so," but he, being an engineering student, said, "you need to learn to study and spend *hours* at the library. You need to stay there until the library closes."

I'd never heard of such a concept. But after working on study tips and note-taking skills, my grades improved dramatically. This was the first time that I earned a 4.0. This guy Herman sure was special. We married right after I graduated.

One of the most important things I learned about this wonderful man was that he had a great love for God and His Word. We prayed together, attended church together, and continued to work on our career plans. Within a few months, we took over raising my son, moved into our first home, and started our family. Over the next few years, we had three more children, and we found jobs in Oklahoma City and later in Tulsa.

Shortly after our fourth child was born, Herman received the opportunity to work for Hughes Aircraft in Carlsbad, California; we decided to move from Oklahoma to North San Diego County in 1986, which was one of the best decisions we could have made.

The opportunity for job training and advancement, along with our children receiving a great education, was a win-win for our young family. Our children were educated in predominantly white, middle-class neighborhoods because Herman and I wanted our kids to be comfortable in America's main-stream society. Herman eventually became a test engineer—an occupation that he greatly enjoyed. A few years later we had our fifth and final child—Gerald.

Now as parents of five children, we acknowledged that we weren't perfect. But we still tried to raise our children with the same principles that I had learned as a child. These principles later carried me through one of the hardest things I ever had to do—to let go of my child after he committed suicide.

~~

Gerald was born and spent his early years in Southern California, which is nothing like living in the South. We didn't realize that when we moved back to the South—a region embedded with systemic racial prejudice—it was going to be a game-changer for him.

Gerald was in elementary school when we moved from Southern California to North Texas. It was then that we noticed our once bubbly child had become more somber. Was he despondent because he had moved from an embracing community in California to the stand-offish behavior of our neighbors in Texas? If so, his response to the attitudes he was beginning to encounter was difficult for me to grasp. From my way of thinking, another person's attitude has no bearing on my own. Had I not taught this concept sufficiently to him? We wondered if Gerald's negative thoughts were the result of the way he was now being treated.

This led me to realize that Black American children growing up in middle-class America may not be sufficiently equipped to handle covert racism. It doesn't resonate with them that there might be an underlying foundation to a bigoted individual's response or attitude when you engage with them. However, I never realized that a child's illogical and depressing thoughts could prove to be deadly.

I remember one day reflecting on all the ways we had encouraged and worked with our children and thought, "We sure raised this last child right." Gerald was a talented musician who could sing harmony with the best of them in his beautiful baritone voice. Not only could he read music, but he had also taught himself to play the piano and guitar. He was a gifted baseball player. He always performed above average in public school, and as a ninth grader, he was accepted into one of the top private schools in the country. Even though he had so much going for him, for some reason, he still felt inadequate.

After seeking answers from several medical professionals, the official diagnosis came: Gerald suffered from depression. Depression is an illness that eats away at an individual's self-esteem and the ability to crawl out of despair. Once the specialist recognized Gerald's depression and prescribed medication to help him, our family went on a different journey emotionally. We found ourselves always "waiting for the other shoe to drop" because the negative side effects of the medication included excessive mood swings. How could we keep Gerald engaged and moving forward in school, athletics, music—in life? Which school would he feel most comfortable in and find self-confidence and success? Public school wasn't the answer. Private school didn't seem to be the answer either. But praise God he finally graduated from high school through a self-study program and began to attend junior college in the summer of 2008.

Once Gerald graduated, my husband and I started to work on our post-graduate degrees; I was so excited to see what my next venture in life would be.

From what we could see, things were looking up for Gerald. He'd recently reached out to a counselor at a local junior college to be re-admitted so that he could continue his college education. He was set to begin a new course of study once enrollment opened for that next semester. A week before his death, he called me and asked what he should do about his relationship with his girlfriend. I drove over to his apartment and spent time talking to both of them about their communication conflicts. I later took him aside privately and gave him options to consider if they moved forward as a couple.

A few days before he died, Gerald called me again to talk about their relationship. We discussed possible alternatives for his future that he could consider.

Hours before his death, Gerald sent me a text at 2 a.m.: "I love you mom and dad." When I awoke that day and saw the text, I didn't think it was unusual because we often told each other how much we loved each other.

It was 9:30 a.m. when two police officers came to our home.

"Mrs. Dade? We want to talk to you about Gerald." They asked if they could enter the house. As I led them inside the living room to have a seat, I wondered what Gerald had gotten himself into.

One of the officers apologized and said, "I'm sorry to inform you that your son has died."

My mind must have short circuited because I remember the officer moving his lips, but I didn't understand what he was saying. But then the reality of his words must have suddenly hit me because I remember slamming myself to the back of my chair. One officer sprang toward me with his lips moving. Not hearing what he was saying, I realized he must have been concerned about how I was receiving the information.

It was then that our family life as I knew it changed forever.

I'll never forget hearing the last words the officer told me that Gerald spoke: "Tell my mom and my dad that I love them." This was while he was sitting on the railing of a Dallas freeway overpass. The police officers begged him to choose life. Gerald chose death.

Then he jumped.

~~~~~

I must have had my cell phone in my hand when the officers were in our home because my next thought was that I needed to call my husband.

Herman is my rock. But when I got him on the phone, I was all choked up and could barely squeeze out the words.

"Honey, Gerald is no longer with us. The police are here with me now."

"Hold on," he replied. "I'll be right there."

Does it make sense that Gerald believed that death would make his hurt go away? How could such a talented individual believe that being dead was better than being alive?

I realized that I now had to call our four children—one of the hardest things I've ever done, but it was the next step forward that I needed to take. When I told them that Gerald had taken his life, each of them broke down in tears but comforted my heart by saying they would be on their way home as soon as possible.

It was a great blessing to have many friends and family members rally around my husband and me to help us make it through the rest of that life-changing week. We were not given the opportunity to sit in despair but were encouraged and comforted as we made plans to do something that no parent ever wants to do—to plan a memorial service for their beloved child.

All the values that my parents had instilled in me, along with what I had learned from my Christian faith, helped me to start believing that my family and I were going to eventually be okay. But it sure would be a difficult journey getting there.

Before twenty-four hours had passed, many in my extended family called and then began to arrive at our house. I was floored when my youngest brother took leave from his job, shopped for groceries, cooked up the best fried chicken dinner this side of heaven, and then drove many miles to bring it to our house. He was my mainstay for many days and even fielded questions from my neighbors, which soothed my heart. I didn't have any answers anyway.

My twenty-three-year-old son had committed suicide, and I was caught up trying to figure out the *why* of such a final act. As a parent, I wondered why my son didn't reach out to us more often if things were so bad. Though he'd suffered from depression for some time, he seemed to have adjusted to his life and had told us about some positive experiences he was having. He had once remarked that he didn't like to take his medication for his depression because "it makes me too sleepy." You can't make an able-bodied adult do something they don't want to do. How were we to know that his decision not to take his medication was the beginning of the end of his life? How do you convince your grown son that he is in a toxic relationship which isn't sustainable or that he's employed in a field that doesn't use his strengths to their fullest?

I don't believe that there is a single person or event to blame for a person's suicide because it usually takes years to bring about a self-inflicted ending. One destructively errant thought left unchecked will often fester. Perhaps the person sees no end to their hurt and decides they've had enough.

Suicide is death on more than one level. It's the death of dreams unrealized and plans gone astray. Death's tentacles stretch out to affect all the loved ones left behind. Some more than others. The glue of love once binding the family together falls apart because the organic structure of a family changes abruptly. The lasting effects of a suicide remain for many years.

If we knew the day that we would leave this earth, what would we do with those last moments with those we love? Would we spend all night together watching that movie we'd been promising each other we'd watch for years? Or would we sit quietly holding each other tightly and waiting for that last breath? Losing a loved one to mental illness often happens with no warning. And we certainly didn't expect this to happen to our child. All our future plans for helping him navigate adulthood suddenly went up in smoke.

There is no closure to a suicide. There is no understandable "why" to the loss of such a precious life. If a loved one suffered from a terminal physical illness and died, the "why" is the disease. If the loved one died due to a fatal car crash, the "why" is the car crash. Likewise for a murder, or poisoning, or old age. When you lose a brother, sister, wife, husband or child to suicide, the loved ones left behind continually question the "why." When Gerald died, I asked myself, "Didn't my son love me? Wasn't I enough?"

It was unfathomable to me that the sweat and tears through the years of attempting to raise a healthy, well-rounded individual in a loving family ended so harshly. I was left to endure the cycle of disbelief, denial, resolution, grief, anger, and ultimately acceptance.

To help my psyche, I knew that I now needed to take some steps that would help me heal. I took my steps slowly—one at a time. All I told myself to do was to keep taking the next step.

I had to figure out what I could do to live with my grief and how to get my life back together. At first, it didn't feel like I *could* do those things. It was easy to see how grief could lead to depressive thoughts. These thoughts allowed my emotions to get the best of me. I couldn't stop crying. Others in my situation might yell or scream, which are also appropriate responses. I needed to do whatever I could do to get my emotions verbalized so that I could move forward.

Having felt that I'd shed enough tears to feel a bit better, I then knew that I had to keep moving forward. Picking my trampled heart up off the floor, the first thought I had was, "Maybe I could help someone else. Perhaps other moms were going through some crisis or a tragedy and could use my support." This thought started my path on a new trajectory in a field I later came to love—youth engagement.

I registered to be a substitute teacher at the local school district and asked to be sent to Title 1 Schools. Those families were the ones I felt could really use my help because their demographics were fraught with low-income housing and with people living at the poverty level. I felt the leadership development programs I had been a part of, coupled with my master's degree in Human Resource Training and Development, would help me succeed as a teacher.

I certainly had a rude awakening! Finding a way to help these kids was not easy.

One morning some students were giving me all kinds of grief. I was trying to call roll, and students were answering for others, starting fights, and throwing pencils across the room. I'd only gotten halfway through the list before I felt like running out of the room crying. I stopped calling roll and looked down at the list, staring at the next name. I prayed for strength until I had composed myself. Oddly enough, the room fell quiet. I was able to continue.

That experience taught me to get a smarter plan to help those who seem to want no help. Do these students truly want a better life, or are they just lashing out to see who has the guts to help them get better? After that day, I did two things. I changed my attitude about these students and started calling them my "little darlings." I also enrolled in the teacher preparation program with Texas Teachers.

This was when I realized I had more questions and more decisions to make: *How can I make a difference? How can I honor my son? Would I allow myself to remain in grief and inaction, or would I do what needed to be done, which was to help motivate as many of these struggling students as I could?* They needed a fighting chance, and I was committed to helping them find their voices.

It's amazing that once you make a decision, you start to notice signposts to guide your steps toward making that decision take root.

One day I stumbled upon a Texas county initiative to alleviate the local truancy problem. This innovative program called for community volunteers to have face-to-face meetings with parents and their students to discuss their numerous absences and tardies. After going through the necessary training, I realized how difficult it was to understand the youth in our schools and why they often act the way they do. They are trying to fit into a culture which their parents may believe is easy to live in. But so many things can send a student into a tailspin. I was counseled about what red flags to look for. I learned that I was good at listening to a young person's life story.

Shortly after I started volunteering, I was asked to join this organization as a part-time case manager. This was my new calling—helping students who have so many challenges to realize and pursue their dreams.

Through these painful years since Gerald committed suicide, I've learned that everyone potentially has the strength to rise up and be the person he or she wants to be. If I could have a positive effect on these kids' lives, maybe they could feel the hope that Gerald never felt. My son didn't die in vain.

~~~

When you are healing from trauma, there are *many* times you need the peace and quiet serenity of listening to your own breath. Taking those cleansing breaths in and out often reminded me that *I* was still alive, which was a good thing. That air allowed me to dream of ways that I could honor my son and live the life he would have wanted me to live had he still been with us. Most importantly, it allowed me to construct ways I could help other families who suffered from a similar tragedy.

But this was also not the time to remain alone. Another important step to my healing was staying in contact with my true friends and family members who wanted to help me carry my load. As I made phone calls to close friends and family members, they took me under their wings. I didn't know it at the time, but it took a while before I could talk about my loss. At the time, I felt like I was punched in the stomach, and there was no air to breathe. It felt like there was a very heavy burden on my back that I just couldn't carry. I'm not sure what was happening to my body, but the result made it hard to move, similar to walking in deep wet sand at the beach while carrying a heavy load. Each step I took was a chore.

Thankfully, I was blessed with a large family and a tremendous number of friends and neighbors who constantly asked what they could do for me. The closest of my friends and family members knew that the best thing they could do was to sit quietly with me and listen without asking questions or giving advice.

Studying God's Word also helped me a great deal during this time. Through my reading, I realized that freedom of will can be man's greatest blessing, or it can be used to destroy a person's soul and wreak havoc on them. While my son's death was devastating to my heart, my zest for life provided me with a quiet victory. Out of my loss, God continued to teach me that I needed to keep inspiring others to live.

A few months after our son passed, Herman and I learned that we had an insurance policy on Gerald through Herman's job that we didn't realize was there. With the money from it, we decided to set up a scholarship designated for at-risk students at the local community college. We also added an account at our bank where anyone outside our family could donate money in Gerald's memory to help these students.

How does a person move on from such a devastating loss? There is no moving on, but there is living with the loss and making each day count. You can recover a person's lost dreams by making a difference in someone else's life. You can help another family find its way before it experiences a devastating loss. You can guide a young person on the path to realizing his or her potential. You can honor the memory of your great times together by waking up and living life each day to its fullest. You must shake off the grief that clings and accumulates until its weight almost breaks you. If you don't do this, the loss you experienced will result in you losing another life—your own.

Not a day or week passes without me remembering my son's little quirks and idiosyncrasies. Sometimes I will hear one of his favorite songs or see a friend of his, and the hurt feels like he took his life yesterday.

My emotions still erupt at any given moment, which results in both laughter or tears. But with God's help, I've learned to be okay with not understanding the illogic of a beautiful life that ended way too soon.

In January 2022, my husband and I, along with two of our children and their spouses, traveled to Oceanside, California, to bury Gerald's ashes at sea. What a poignant reminder this was of his greatest desire—to return home to California. It took us nine years to honor his request.

A brother of mine comforted me once with these words, "The pain doesn't stop hurting once you lose a child, but living life does get easier."

Losing a child takes your breath away. I'm still trying to get it fully back.

"CRY, CRY"

LEANNE MERTZMAN

Sometimes the bathroom floor is inevitable. It's been that way lately at my house. I wait until my wife and our two daughters fall asleep, until the house is quiet, and the only thing left to do is to let the day finally catch up to me. That's when I sit down on the cold, hard tiles of my bathroom floor, drop my head, and let myself fall apart. The worst part is knowing that when I get up, the misery of today is only going to repeat itself. I have no idea what the next day will bring, no telling when all this will end. There is no light at the end of the tunnel. So I sob. By my mid-thirties, I've given up on trying to fight it. Fighting the tears is fruitless. I'm old enough to know that if I need to cry, I should let myself cry until there are no tears left.

It's cancer that broke me. Not even my own. My wife's. She and I are both strong women; we've had to be. And it's both a blessing and a curse in our lives. We met when we were twenty-four and living in Los Angeles. We fell in love fast and hard, like they do in the movies. At the time we got married, only a handful of states allowed same-sex couples to marry, and our home state of California wasn't one of them.

Instead, we did the closest thing we could to marriage—we registered as domestic partners, invited a hundred of our friends, and had our wedding anyway. Complete with a rabbi, a Lutheran pastor, and a mix of traditions from our separate faiths, we promised to love each other in sickness and in health, through thick and through thin, no matter what may come. And we sure have done so.

Allison and I are rock solid communicators. It's my favorite part of our marriage. We listen to each other, we constantly work to change our behaviors in ways that work better for each other, we apologize frequently, and we forgive and forget.

Allison is easily my best and favorite friend. Our language is primarily made up of inside jokes and movie quotes, and our happy place is watching our five favorite romantic comedies together on the couch. Our marriage thrives because we promise to wake up every day and choose each other.

Then cancer hit, and neither of us wanted to wake up at all.

Allison was diagnosed with Stage 2 metastatic ductal carcinoma on a Tuesday morning in 2021. What a shitty way to wake up. The whole thing happened so fast, although I don't think she'd describe it that way. In a week she'd undergone a mammogram, then an ultrasound, and finally a biopsy. Luckily, her doctors worked quickly to provide her with answers.

"Babe, my doctor's on the phone; do you want to be here for this?" Typing this memory still sends chills up my spine. I can hear her defeated voice ask me, both of us knowing bad news was imminent. I grabbed my glasses and followed her back to our kitchen table. Whatever it was, we'd face it together.

By the end of the conversation, Allison was hysterical. Rightfully so, because we found out her treatment regimen would include chemotherapy. She would face an Everest level of torture and trauma to her body and be practically poisoned in her own skin. That's what chemotherapy is—battling toxins by drowning your body with other toxins and hoping that you kill the cancer toxins before they kill you.

Allison's chemotherapy was scheduled in three-week cycles. Day one was the actual chemotherapy infusion, where Allison would get pumped full of Taxotere, Carboplatin, Herceptin, and Perjeta. There'd be another day or two where she'd maybe feel close to normal, but by day three, it was hell on earth for her. Fevers, hot flashes, vomiting, aching, canker sores, hives, constipation, diarrhea—a grab-bag of crappy potential side effects—and Allison was one of those lucky people who got them all. Hell would go on through week one and all the way through week two. With most rounds of chemo (she had six in total), she'd have a few days where she felt well enough to get out of the house or to work for several hours at a time. But inevitably, day one would come again, and the roulette of symptoms started over.

Our rule was that on the good days, we never talked about the looming chemotherapy appointment; not until the night before when we got out the heated blankets and the ice packs would we admit it, even though we both knew it had never really stopped haunting us.

During those two-week periods when my wife was sick beyond belief in our bedroom, I felt like half of my world was gone. Our marriage had been strong and collaborative, so our parenting was too. We always prioritized parenting as a team, taking care to never undermine each other and always presenting a united front to our children. We'd both been working remotely due to Covid, but we'd managed our schedules well to split parenting duties and accommodate both of our jobs. I worked during the day as a lawyer while Allison covered the kids' school drop-offs and activities. Then I took over at dinner to cover bath and bedtime with them so Allison could have a few hours to manage her travel agency. Allison made dinner and the school lunches. I did the dishes and laundry. We had the whole thing down pat.

Cancer blew it all to bits. When Allison started chemotherapy, she became a ghost, evidenced only by the blue plastic barf bags lining our hallways.

Anyone who's been in love knows the brutality of watching your partner in pain. There were days when her skin was yellow and others where she was so pale and so frail it was like she'd aged a decade. She'd hobble from the bed to the kitchen for more ice or more meds, and then back to the bedroom for another eight hours. Some days she didn't see our kids at all. Those were the days that always ended with me in a fetal position on the bathroom floor.

I don't lie to my kids. There was one time I got myself into a jam about Santa Claus which necessitated some creative fibbing, but mostly, I'm honest with my tiny humans.

They've known that their moms are gay, that some people are assholes about it, and yes, they know the word "asshole" even though they're four and six. They're bright, young girls, and I know they're going to learn all the "adult" words eventually, so I figure I might as well define them correctly when they ask. They know that their biological father was a sperm donor, that one of them was conceived using my egg and another with Allison's, and that Allison gave birth to both of them. We've made it a priority to always be as honest with them as possible in an age-appropriate way.

There's no good way to say, "Your mom will be sick as fuck for four months" to your elementary-age daughters. We found books that explained radiation and chemo to children, but with my kids, explanations only begat more questions. They learned the mechanics of what was happening in Mommy's body, how chemo would fight the bad cells, and how that would make Mommy not feel like Mommy for a while. But they couldn't grasp the "why" of it all, and I don't blame them. Nothing about it was fair. It wasn't fair that some days Mommy's body was too weak and bruised too easily even for hugs. It wasn't fair that Mommy missed out on Thanksgiving, Hanukkah, Christmas, or that she had chemotherapy on New Year's Day.

So, I'd hold them, and I'd hear their feelings. I'd tell them it was okay to be sad—that I was sad, too. I'd tell them that today was hard but that they survived it and that we only had to worry about this one day at a time. I'd tell them that someday we wouldn't feel this mad or this sad, and that they are allowed to feel their feelings. I'd let them cry themselves to sleep in my arms, and then the house would fall silent, and it would finally be my turn to cry.

Cancer made me nearly hate Allison. Now I realize that, of course, it was the cancer I hated, but it took the form of Allison for its residency. I hated that she was sick. I hated that she was depressed and morbid and a ball of anxiety. I hated that my best friend was gone. I lost my parenting teammate and my wife, the woman who used to let me hug and kiss her and put my hands on her body when she walked by me. Cancer made me afraid to touch her as I might wound her. Allison missed out on life for weeks at a time, and when she would arise from the dead, it was impossible for her to catch up on work, on TV shows or current events, or even on the girls' daily lives. On the "good nights," Allison would cry herself to sleep, too; she'd feel heartbroken for not spending time with the kids when her work was urgent. Then she'd feel equally guilty for not responding to clients when she chose time with her daughters instead.

Thankfully, we were so blessed to have family and friends help in every possible way. Allison's parents moved into town and took on the role of chauffeur, driving her to and from her endless slew of appointments. The rest of our immediate family tried to stagger their visits so that we'd have extra hands on deck at all times to help with school drop-offs and pick-ups.

Our village rallied to send us food delivery gift cards and bring us homemade meals. During the days, we had a schedule to maintain, a calendar full of appointments to get to. But nighttime would come, and at nighttime, it was just the four of us. Which meant that at nighttime, for all intents and purposes, it was just me.

During Cancer—we use the capital-C word to refer to the entire time period now— the girls had bigger emotions to process and more energy than usual to expel, all of which seemed to explode during what we dubbed "the witching hour." Baths turned into water splashing fights or actual fights that resulted in soaked floors. Soaked floors meant more wet towels, meant more laundry; more laundry meant less sleep.

Every action resulted in a bigger and worse reaction. I'd stay awake late to watch a TV show to try to feel like my world wasn't crumbling for twenty-two minutes, and I'd end up forgetting to pack a kid's lunch the next morning. It felt like no matter what decision I made, someone in the family suffered. And me being who I am, that person was usually me.

As Allison progressed through chemotherapy, my daughters started to realize how badly it was destroying their mom...s. Allison's physical side effects were cumulative, and they rippled through the rest of us. My daughters weren't sleeping well; I could see them start to internalize Allison's behavior—her short temperedness and crankiness on the days she was sick, her distractedness on the days she wasn't. There were fewer nights we were able to go in and gently say goodnight to her, and the lack of time spent with Allison meant that all my kids' rage was directed at me. I watched them become more anxious as they understood more, and then, I felt at fault for having been honest with them.

Allison was practically overcome with fear—fear that the chemo wouldn't work, that the cancer had spread, that catching Covid might kill her. And then there was me—a shell of the person I used to be. I wasn't eating, barely sleeping, still trying to pretend I was holding it together. I tried to remind myself that Allison would finish chemotherapy at some point, but chemo was only the first part of a three-pronged attack; Allison still had breast surgery and radiation to go. I couldn't see light at the end of the tunnel. My lawyer brain couldn't come up with any way to spin this into something positive. That little voice inside me that reminds me to never give up—that points out the good in things—was gone.

I was hopeless. And it scared the hell out of me.

Some days the only thing I could manage to do was to put one foot in front of the other; on those days, I tried my hardest to let that be enough.

～

That's how it was when our second daughter was born in 2018, a few years after I'd finished law school. Our oldest, Ruthie, was two, and since she had been born prematurely, Allison's second pregnancy was categorized as "high risk." Allison had weekly ultrasounds to track her progress; and then, at her twenty-week scan, we found out something was terribly wrong.

It was the one ultrasound I didn't accompany Allison to. Instead, I was walking across the parking garage on my way into my office when Allison called.

"There's something wrong with the baby's heart, but they aren't sure what it is," she sobbed into the phone.

I headed across town, conjuring up every worst-case scenario in my head, and I was only able to wrap my wife in a quick hug before they sent us to a cardiology hospital for a fetal echocardiogram.

"Whatever it is, we'll handle it together," I told Allison. It wasn't much, but I don't lie to my wife either. It was the only thing I could say with any certainty. I didn't know if everything would be okay. As it turned out, it wasn't.

Transposition of the Great Arteries—"TGA" as it's known—is a fluke. It's a rare congenital heart defect that affects 1 in every 5,000 babies. The fetal heart begins in the shape of a tube, and as it develops, it performs a number of twists and turns that normally result in the anatomy of the healthy human heart: four chambers—left and right atrium, left and right ventricle—and two main arteries—the aorta that pumps blood to the body, and the pulmonary artery that pumps blood to the lungs. Our baby's heart failed to make one of the last twists, so her aorta and her pulmonary artery ended up in the wrong places: reversed.

In a heart with TGA, the aorta and the pulmonary artery are attached to the opposite ventricles; thus, they send blood to the wrong place. So instead of flowing in the shape of a figure eight through the heart, blood flows in two independent circles: a heart-lungs loop and a body-heart loop. As a result, the body doesn't get oxygen as it should, so babies born with TGA actually come out looking purple. While we found out about our daughter's heart condition early because of Allison's many cautious ultrasounds, roughly half the time new parents don't find out about their child's TGA until the baby comes out with a violet hue—like our Rosie did. I've got the pictures in my phone to prove it.

It was an unbelievably hard day, but finding out about Rosie's congenital heart defect in advance turned out to be helpful for us. Those extra months gave us time to prepare.

We saw a number of specialists and toured hospitals. We were hell-bent on getting the best care possible and fortunate to have the resources to make it happen. But learning about the problem early on gave us extra months to panic. We were bringing a child with a messed-up heart into this world, one who we learned would need open heart surgery in order for her to have a chance at a healthy, viable life.

Without medical intervention on standby to provide oxygen, our baby wouldn't be able to survive for more than a few minutes. She'd need constant care in the Pediatric Intensive Care Unit until surgery. And then, to permanently correct the anatomy of her heart by switching her tiny arteries back to the right place, Rosie would need open-heart surgery shortly after birth.

Rosie was born in an operating room at 9:01 a.m. in Michigan on a cold March day. I stood there in my paper gown, terrified from the second she was born. She didn't cry at all at first, not until Allison urged her gently, "Cry, cry," and Rosie listened. I cut her umbilical cord, and then Allison held her for two minutes. I spent the entirety of those two minutes silently panicking.

She's losing oxygen. Is she losing too much oxygen? My mind raced. I felt the tears streak down my face as I watched Allison hold Rosie, and I kept glancing at the doctor's eyes, watching for any sign that anything was wrong. It's a panic that still lives in my gut, a visceral reminder of the weight of parenting. Our newborn would have to get her heart cut open and sewn back together, and I wouldn't be able to do any of the hard part for her. All I could do was stand by and watch.

I watched as the doctors finally took Rosie back—and then they shuffled her one room over and strapped her to a hospital table. I followed her into the sterile room and watched the nurses jam IV lines into her belly button—the "easiest" place for an arterial line, they told me. They covered her chest with little stickers and then clipped heart monitors to them. From that second, she would be bound for nearly a month by beeping monitors and an annoying arterial line. She screamed as they poked and prodded her; to this day, her crying haunts my nightmares. When she finally fell asleep, I noticed her little wrists had imprints of the medical straps, shackles basically, that they'd needed to hold her down. My one-hour old was facing torture in front of me, while my wife lay on a hospital bed a room behind me, and my other daughter waited down the hall with her grandmother. My three girls. I couldn't help any of them.

I felt worthless, helpless, hopeless, and scared out of my mind. I cried so much that first day—I'm confident it was the fastest I've ever gone through a full box of Kleenex.

At thirteen days old, Rosie had her arterial switch operation. Doctors performed a sternotomy and cut open her chest. They lowered her temperature and her heart rate, put her on bypass, and then they cut open her heart. Rosie was a few weeks premature, so she was only about six pounds with a heart the size of a piece of ravioli. But a brilliant cardio-thoracic surgeon was able to repair it, moving her tiny little arteries around, carefully snipping and reattaching them where they belonged. And eventually Rosie's chest was sewn up, and her puzzle-piece heart started beating just like mine.

The days after surgery were excruciating. Babies return from their operations with so many bruises, bandages, cords, and wires that the nurses arranged for us to visit another couple's post-op child a few days before Rosie's surgery to help manage our expectations. I took pictures of everything—I needed to document even the worst days because I knew that someday Rosie would need to hear and see what she had been through. I photographed the incremental healing of the massive scar across her chest, the feeding tubes in her nose, and the ventilator. I photographed even the things they told me not to, like the x-ray machine for infants which looked like a medieval torture device.

Someday this will all be behind us, I prayed. *Decades from now these will be photos in an old album on my phone and stories to tell Rosie over a cup of coffee.*

~⌇~

During Rosie's time in the hospital, managing everything was impossible; actually, managing anything was impossible. Allison was still recovering from the effects of giving birth, and Ruthie was a toddler, scared for her baby sister and learning how to sleep in a new place without both moms. I had been working for my company less than twelve months and wasn't eligible for paid parental leave, so I worked remotely. I sat in a wobbly green chair beside Rosie's hospital bed and reviewed contracts at three in the morning. I drafted responses to all my emails and waited to hit "send" until the daytime hours. Work, at least, provided a brief distraction from all the unknowns sitting heavy on my chest—we didn't know how long Rosie would be in the hospital, what limitations she'd have when we took her home, or if we'd get to take her home at all.

Many of those nights I did my crying while simultaneously holding Rosie's hand. I'd put the hoodie of my sweatshirt up, let the tears fall, and the nurses on the nightshift knew nothing needed to be said about it. At night, when the hospital was calm and the cardio wing was dimly lit, I'd let myself fall apart. I'd let it all out so that I could keep going.

It took me thirty years to learn how to cry in public. I used to prefer crying in the shower, alone, the steady flow of water wiping away any evidence of my doubt or my debilitating fear. During Rosie's time in the hospital, there was no shower for me to escape into, and during Cancer, I rarely had the time for a lengthy crying session in the shower anyway—a kid or a wife always needed something at a moment's notice. Crying in the shower had been a privilege of my youth; it was a way to hide away my embarrassment and shame from the world.

As an adult, I've realized there's no point in hiding my tears. It's good, it's right to let them out. It felt natural on those nights and in the days after chemo to crumple over on the floor and ball up in the fetal position rather than stand up straight. I had no control. I wasn't fooling myself into thinking I'd walk away feeling clean or refreshed. I knew damn well I'd eventually get up off the floor with snot all over the nearest towel or my shirt, with no more knowledge and no better outlook than I'd previously had. After wasting a precious hour, I'd go back to piles of laundry with another dirty shirt to add to the mix. I'd return to a house that felt overwhelming, a life that felt crushing. I'd leave the bathroom with nothing more than I'd come in with, save for tear-stained cheeks.

Good thing tear-stained cheeks are my superpower.

I must have cried thousands of times, in hundreds of places across the span of my life. Little me cried when I crashed my Big Bird Big Wheel at the bottom of the driveway and when I used to fall out of the cherry trees in the front yard. I wept as a teenager when my parents got divorced and when my young heart got broken the first time. I shed tears after zillions of tough sports losses throughout the years and during the times I got cut from the team. Plenty of tears were

113

caused by all the assholes and all the shitty homophobic comments I've heard during my thirty-six years in this skin.

But I've survived all of it.

Every single second of it.

Whatever the words were that hurt me, I survived. Every time I started crying, I eventually stopped. Every morning that I wasn't sure whether I had the strength to make it through the day, I made it. I have resoundingly and overwhelmingly survived. I did good. I'm *doing* good. Sometimes I need reminding.

Take a breath. *We're all doing good.*

Even on the days when our faces are red and splotchy, when we feel hopeless and buried under an avalanche, we're still doing good. Our resilience is written all over our faces on those days because it's on those days that we endure. Anyone can get through a joyous, happy day; the hard days are when we're at our strongest. Crying is evidence of our living. Of our surviving.

"Cry, cry." Sometimes I hear Allison's sweet, scared voice encouraging me.

Crying is the first thing we do, the first sign of life to our mothers. It's a letting go and a giving up. And it's okay to give up sometimes. It's okay to wallow, to let life eat you alive for a few minutes. I'm the type of person who likes to be fully informed; I want to know and understand every potential outcome, the variables that may impact things, and everything in between. I must be able to see all of it to plan for it. And when I'm operating in "emergency mode"—as I was most of the year of Allison's Cancer—I needed to be able to plan for everything. Cancer is *Cancer*. It required surgeries and going under and lymphotomies and lumpectomies and about a million needles going into my wife. There were PET scans, MRIs, ultrasounds, and never-ending bloodwork, and Allison went in every time fearing the worst: the treatment hadn't or wouldn't work. She was terrified that she was going to die; during the roughest weeks she couldn't talk about anything else. It was my job to stay positive for her and for our girls. But there were times I needed to let myself go to the most terrifyingly dark place. It was always a fear, so in order to move past it, I needed to let myself feel it. If the absolute worst-case scenario happened and we lost Allison, I wouldn't be able to fall apart; the girls would need their other parent more than anything else in the world.

So at nights, I'd let the darkest fears take over. I'd feel it all deep in my bones, and I'd cry until I'd cried through all my feelings. Life is indescribably painful at times, and it doesn't help anyone to pretend like it isn't. It's okay to rage, panic, or check out. It's okay to do the bare minimum. To have off days. To grieve your pre-trauma life as long as you need to. It's okay to say, "fuck it all" and take a mental health day, drive yourself to the beach, and sit in your car to weep uncontrollably for an afternoon. It's okay to do whatever the thing is that takes you back to equilibrium, no matter how trivial or inexplicable it may seem.

Sometimes for me it's a puzzle, or a LEGO set, or a nighttime drive. I'll let myself get lost listening to a new playlist, then try to find my way back home sans-Waze. A few nights in the hospital with Rosie, I found myself playing with Ruthie's Play-Doh after she'd left, needing to squeeze something in my hands in an attempt to maintain some semblance of control.

There was a month during Allison's chemotherapy when I made friendship bracelets in the little time I had to myself. Like a middle schooler, I sat on the couch braiding colored strings together in heart patterns because it temporarily took my mind off my life. It's okay to insist on time for self-care; in fact, it's necessary in order to be a good caregiver. I couldn't help support my partner or my family when I couldn't hold myself up first.

Part of holding myself up meant leaning on others, something that doesn't come easily to me during a time of crisis. But when people offered to bring food, I let them, and when friends and acquaintances asked how we were doing, I answered honestly. I let them share the emotional load of my life for a minute so that I could maintain a positive attitude around Allison and our kids.

When my friends called to check in on me, I always answered the phone. My wife calls this "grieving out"—I was so much more emotionally available to Allison when I had verbally longed for my pre-cancer life to friends other than Allison. I tried to be an upbeat and willing caregiver, but on the days I failed to stay positive—and there were plenty—I forgave myself and vowed to try again tomorrow. It's okay to get it wrong. It's okay to not be perfect.

On the days I didn't check everything off my list, which was most days, I was still doing okay. Sometimes life is a to-do list that never ends and a bed that I never get to sleep in. Sometimes a solution is something as simple as a laundry service. During the Cancer days, laundry was everywhere. I think at one point we had seven rotating laundry bins. Seven, for a house with four people. They were every where and crippling. They were the visual representation of my internal state of mind, like icons busying up the desktop of my vision.

As soon as I came up for air, I figured out a way to carve sixty-five dollars a week out of our monthly budget. Now our laundry gets picked up every Monday and dropped off every Tuesday. I may not be able to banish dirty clothes from my house in entirety, but I won't be drowning alive underneath them.

On the days I still feel underwater, it's okay to live life one day, one hour, or even one minute at a time. When I feel myself start to spiral in moments of grief or depression or panic, I take a deep breath and remind myself to "be where my feet are." I try to remember that it wasn't always like this.

Then I pray that it won't always be.

These days, Rosie is nearly five and has no physical limitations. You'd never know—lots of her friends don't know—that she had open heart surgery when she was two weeks old. They don't know she spent a total of twenty-eight days in the hospital, that she was discharged three days shy of what was supposed to be her due date. They see a rambunctious kid, a chatterbox who narrates everything she does, a fearless girl who wears fancy dresses to play in the dirt. Rosie has yearly cardiology visits, echocardiograms, and other tests to check her heart function—visits which have gotten progressively easier as she's grown.

There's a possibility of Rosie needing further surgeries somewhere down the road, and it's not all roses as the effects of those first days strapped to a hospital bed rather than being cuddled by her moms will continue to be a source of trauma. But all four of our hearts are still

117

beating, so for now I'll hold them all tightly and thankfully, and I'll continue to take it one day at a time.

For her part, Allison is Cancer-free and a changed woman in so many ways.

"Cancer-free, but not worry-free," she tells me. Six rounds of chemo, thirty-three days of radiation, breast surgery and a reduction, followed by lots of physical therapy. Still, over a year out from her diagnosis in September of 2021, she has some days when her energy wanes and some days when she's sore or uncomfortable. But mostly, she's her vibrant self. She came back to life three cup sizes smaller and even more passionate and true to herself than she was before.

Allison will always worry that her cancer might return. It left her with Post Traumatic Stress Disorder as a constant reminder of her year of hell, and we and both kids are in individual therapy to help process all of what we've been through. As soon as Allison started feeling better physically, she was ready to take on the world and make up for lost time; I, on the other hand, was physically exhausted and emotionally empty. We had to re-acclimatize to life with each other as we both had changed and grown. But we're doing the hard work to come back to each other.

In sports, this would be called a "rebuilding year." It's hard, and sometimes we screw up. We're human. We still make mistakes. So we give each other the space and the grace to try again. We stand by our promise of a decade ago to take the good with the bad, the sickness with the health, and face whatever comes as a unit. Allison and I are a team that gets bent but is never broken.

Today when I look in the mirror, I see a thirty-six-year-old with eyes less bloodshot than they used to be. I snap a screenshot of myself in my mind and file this image away with the other pictures of me throughout this challenging chapter. I see on some faces the dried tears of my worst days, my absolute hardest moments. A gallery of pictures in my head hangs there to remind me of my strength.

I survived those bathroom floors.

I'll survive the next one, too. I just have to keep getting up.

THE UNHUNG SWING

LESLIE CECHAN

I wanted you to see what real courage is, instead of getting the idea that courage is a man with a gun in his hand. It's when you know you're licked before you begin, but you begin anyway and you see it through no matter what.

—Atticus Finch in *To Kill a Mockingbird*

The swing was never hung. My life was forever changed when my one and only love tragically lost his life on Friday, May 19, 2017.

Donnie and I looked forward to a fun, exciting weekend at the lake house celebrating our grandson's third birthday. We added an extra day to our stay to prepare for our family and festivities. Upon arrival, the truck was unloaded, the dogs were fed, and we took a golf cart ride around our beautiful lake community. Thursday, May 18, 2017, would be our last golf cart ride together.

On Friday morning, Donnie arose from our bed early, eager to begin the day. He never slept late on weekends at the lake. Donnie's fishing pole was always ready for his beloved serene mornings of fishing and sipping coffee. This morning, fishing would have to wait as there were chores to be done before everyone's arrival. The yard was edged, mowed, and blown clean. Weeds were yanked out of the flower beds, and flowers were watered. The deck was sprayed, the flags were hung, and the patio furniture was wiped clean. While Donnie worked his magic outside, I cleaned and freshened up the inside of the lake house before making the Paw Patrol birthday cake celebrating our soon-to-be three-year old grandson.

By early afternoon, Donnie had completed the outside transformation. The yard was lusciously green and ready for bare feet. The golf cart was fully charged and ready for multiple trips around the lake. Only one more job was on the "to do" list—hanging the trampoline swing.

As an engineer, Donnie had planned the best and safest placement for the swing. In our effort to hang the swing, a large, heavy board needed to be secured between two trees. Donnie happened to have the perfect board in his workshop, and he had selected the two trees. The plan was for him to climb up the ladder he had leaning on the side of the tree to temporarily nail up the first end of the board. He would then move to the second tree to secure the board's other end.

"I'm going to climb up to put the first nails in. Can you hold the ladder for me?" he asked.

"Of course!"

"Let's get this side done, and then I'll move to the other tree. Just hold the ladder straight while I nail in this end. After I finish this side,

I'll need you to hold the board up while I move over to the other tree and get that end nailed into the tree. Try not to let the board fall."

"I'll try. The board is over my head. I can touch it, but I'm not sure I can hold it."

"Okay, Leslie, just try. Use both hands to hold the board while I get the nails in."

With the nails secured to the first tree, Donnie climbed down, grabbed the ladder, and headed to the other tree. The board was inches above my height. Standing on my tiptoes, I could touch the board, but not with enough strength and stability to keep it in place.

Donnie quickly moved to the second tree. With the ladder in place, he climbed up and adjusted the board before nailing it to the tree. But as soon as he adjusted the board, the first side failed, and the board fell to the ground. We found ourselves back at square one.

"I thought you were holding the board!"

"I was until you got to this side and moved it. It was too high for me to hold it!"

"Okay, let's try this again."

Donnie was never one to quit a task. Again, he set up the ladder at the first tree and climbed up to secure the board. I was standing right next to him on the ground, holding the ladder as he reached up to nail the board to the tree.

Suddenly, the ladder twisted, and Donnie slipped and fell off. He knocked me down before he landed hard on the ground, face down on his chest. His glasses flew off and lay in the dirt a few feet away. I picked myself up, retrieved the glasses, and helped Donnie up off the ground. He appeared dazed and was slow to get up.

"Okay, you and I are done for the day," I told him. Donnie mumbled something in response, but he knew we would try to hang it later.

It was late afternoon, the hottest part of the day, the air heavy with humidity. I told Donnie to come inside and I would get him a cool glass of water. We both walked into our lake house, and Donnie sat down at the kitchen table. I went to the refrigerator to fill cups with ice water. When I turned around, Donnie was slumped down in his chair. I ran to him and straightened him up. He was unconscious and non-responsive. In a state of panic, I moved additional chairs together, carefully laid him across the chairs, and began CPR. I do not recall how long I performed CPR…it seemed like forever.

Before long, I grew tired and knew Donnie required more help than I was able to give. I wasn't sure if my CPR efforts were even helping. Was he breathing? Was he still alive? I knew I needed to call for help. This would be my first experience calling 911, and I was terrified. I questioned if my mind was clear enough to relay the information they needed to know. I grabbed my phone.

"911, what is your emergency?"

"It's my husband! I can't tell if he's breathing! I'm trying to do CPR on him."

"Are you alone?"

"Yes, I'm by myself. He fell off a ladder. I can't tell if he's breathing! He needs help now!"

"Okay ma'am, continue administering CPR; don't stop. Help is on the way!"

"Please hurry!"

Our lake house is located within a private fishing lake community in the Piney Woods of East Texas between Palestine and Tyler. The average time it takes to drive to either location from our lake house is approximately thirty minutes. Tyler is the larger of the two cities, and I would want Donnie transported there. I knew a larger city would likely offer more medical services.

The amount of time it took for the paramedics to arrive after the 911 call seemed painfully long. I continued my CPR efforts while pleading with God to keep Donnie alive. Upon arrival, the paramedics bounded in and immediately went to work. Furniture was shoved out of the way, giving the men room.

Cases of medical equipment were brought in. They carefully lifted Donnie off the chairs and placed him on the floor. Sterile medical packages were ripped open. The paramedics worked with their probes, IV's, beeping machines, and other medical devices to help Donnie while I tried to relate the day's events to them. The paramedics worked hard to keep Donnie alive in order to successfully transport him to the hospital.

When it was deemed safe to move Donnie into the ambulance, one of the paramedics asked me, "Ma'am, are you familiar with Palestine?"

"Yes."

"We're taking your husband to Palestine Regional Medical Center. Don't try to follow us. We're gonna drive fast. I suggest you put the address into your GPS."

The ambulance, loaded with paramedics and my most precious Donnie, roared out of the driveway, up through the narrow, curvy road of our lake community with its lights and sirens blaring.

I was now painfully alone, and I was unable to move or process the situation. I looked over the state of the room where these men had worked so intensely to keep Donnie's heart beating. As unsettling as the scene was, I grabbed my car keys. As I drove to Palestine—wishing that I was driving to the larger city, Tyler—I had a hard time seeing the road well due to tears streaming out of my eyes and down my face. I felt so scared. I finally reached the main highway. Sobbing, I called my sister who lives at our lake and tried my best to tell her the horrific details of the afternoon.

"It's me. I need help! Where are you?"

"I'm driving back from College Station. Are you okay? What's wrong?"

Between sobs, I told her the events of the day as best as I could.

"Where are they taking him?"

"To the smaller hospital in Palestine. I'm so scared!"

"Okay, I think I'm pretty close to that hospital. I'll go there and try to find out what's going on. You need to drive carefully. He's in good hands, Leslie. Right now, let's pray."

Sissy prayed the sweetest, heartfelt prayer while we both drove from opposite directions to the hospital. Remarkably, she was closer to Palestine than I and arrived at the hospital before I did. When I arrived, Sissy met me outside in the parking lot, took my hand, and walked me into a small room. A hospital employee explained to us that the doctors and nurses were working hard doing their best to save Donnie.

The long wait began along with all the "what if" scenarios infiltrating my brain. If Donnie needs surgery, who do I contact?

The longing to hear how Donnie was doing was unbearable. Finally, a doctor entered the tiny room and closed the door. He introduced himself and began describing the difficulty they had keeping Donnie's heart beating.

"Due to the fall and the forceful, direct landing on his chest, your husband's heart experienced serious trauma. His heart was having difficulty beating on its own with any regularity. You may have heard of the term, heart arrhythmia. These heart rhythm problems occur when the electrical signals that coordinate the heart's beats don't work properly. Unfortunately, we were not able to get his heart to maintain any sort of rhythm for any length of time without continual intervention. We were never able to restore his heart's normal rhythm. I'm so sorry."

I couldn't believe it! *Was Donnie gone?* How could this happen? What next? I drifted off into some unknown, unfamiliar space. I was aware of another man entering the room. He expressed his condolences and quickly explained what would happen next. I was given a sheet of paper and asked to compose a narrative of the day's events, the worst day of my life. Before I could even manage to gather any rational thoughts, I was reminded it would be most important for me to recall how this horrific day unfolded with as much accuracy as possible. My statement would become an official document.

I was failing miserably at trying to formulate complete thoughts and recall the order of disasters for my statement. Even more arduous was the ability to write the words on this random sheet of paper. My mind was a web of confusion filled to the brink with sadness. My body was trembling. My shaky hand made the simple task of putting words on paper an impossible task. With Sissy's help, I somehow recorded the tragic accident. As challenging as this day had become, it was about to become even more painful and heart wrenching.

I just needed to see Donnie. With the immediate paperwork completed, I asked if I could see my husband. A staff worker arrived and escorted me to see him. As I entered the room, Donnie looked as if he was peacefully sleeping. He had no bruises or cuts. He had on the same clothes he was dressed in earlier in the day. He even still had his glasses on. He wore the beautiful Texas Tech University class ring I had given him for graduation with his wedding band behind it. Oh, and his mustache! In all our years together, I never saw Donnie without his mustache. He often joked with me saying he was hiding an ugly disfigurement. If he shaved the mustache off, I might not love him as much.

Yes, it was still there as it had always been since the first time we met while attending Texas Tech University in Lubbock, Texas. Donnie was a good student, always putting his school responsibilities first. However, when his academic assignments were completed, he was always ready to experience "college life." He made lifelong memories hanging out with his Alpha Tau Omega fraternity brothers. Our first date was a blind date arranged by a friend living on my dorm floor and her boyfriend who lived on Donnie's dorm floor. After that blind date, we continued dating, but because Donnie was such a serious student, many of our dates were in the library. He worked every summer and during spring break to fund his education, and it paid off as we both landed our first jobs right after we graduated. With those goals accomplished, he asked me to marry him.

As tears fell freely from my eyes, I began trying to say good-bye. How does one respond to the tragedy of losing their most beloved life partner? I am certain there is no protocol for this. I had no words, just plenty of tears along with the many wonderful memories we had made together.

I caressed, kissed, and hugged Donnie and told him that I wish we had spent so much more time doing all the things he enjoyed. He loved for me to go fishing with him, even though he always had to bait my hook, and on the rare occasion I caught a fish, remove the catch from my line. Donnie especially loved to take me along on his hunting trips. I always enjoyed going with him even though the drive was long on those endless, flat roads to the deer lease in far west Texas. Once we were settled in the blind in the wee hours of the morning, it was understood there would be no talking. Donnie would softly whisper and point when he would see evidence of a deer approaching. On these hunting excursions, he enjoyed pointing out all the habits, hints, and markings of wildlife. The most exciting trips for both of us were the times when he was able to bring home a deer.

Leaving my one and only love alone in that cold, metallic room was yet another gut-punch. Sissy helped me walk out of the hospital to her car and drove us back to the lake house, both of us numb, in tears, and in shock.

Turning into our driveway we were greeted by an Anderson County officer. I could not understand why all these uniformed men and women continued to question me and why I had to relive the nightmare by telling the story over and over. Little did I know, this was just the beginning.

"Hello, I am here representing the Anderson County Sheriffs' Department. I'm very sorry for your loss. I understand you have had an exhausting day, so I won't take much of your time. I will just need a summary of the events that took place here earlier today starting with the events leading up to the accident and ending with the ambulance leaving for the hospital. I apologize for having to ask you to go through this again. Also, it would be helpful if you could show me where the accident took place."

For the sixth time, I recalled the details and timeline of the day's events, from Donnie describing to me his thoughts on how we would hang the swing, to the disastrous end when Sissy and I returned home from the hospital. I walked the officer to the back of our lake house and up to the tree where it all had started. I pointed out the two trees Donnie had selected, the metal ladder, and the fallen board. His nail gun and work gloves, as well as the unhung swing, still in the box, were all on the ground where we had left them. Sadly, repeating the events of the day now felt mechanical.

When the officer was satisfied with the information I had shared, she took a step back and spoke to me from her heart.

"Mrs. Cechan, I'm so sorry I had to come out here to have you relive this nightmare. This is one part of my job that I don't enjoy. I know you must feel numb right now, and the reality of this situation has not sunk in. I'm going to give you my card. If you find yourself needing someone to talk to or if you have any questions, please do not hesitate to call me. Many days my schedule is flexible. If I'm able, I'd be happy to meet with you. The days to come will be extremely difficult to get through. Do you have any questions for me?"

Frankly, I had so many questions! *Why did this have to happen?* for starters.

"Where is Donnie? What will happen next? Do I make the arrangements to have his body moved?"

"His body will be taken to Forensic Medical Management Services in Tyler, where an autopsy will be performed."

"Why does there need to be an autopsy?"

"Anytime there is an accidental death, the state requires an autopsy. Upon completion of the autopsy, your husband's body will be transported to the funeral home of your choice. Someone will contact you for the name and location of the funeral home you choose."

"How long does it take for an autopsy to be performed?"

"I would say the autopsy could be performed by Monday. His body could possibly be moved later that day. You will be notified when the procedure has been completed and your husband's body is ready to be moved. A written report will be sent to you informing you of the findings and results of the autopsy. Additionally, a death certificate cannot be issued until there is an official cause of death which will be determined from the autopsy. I know this is all very upsetting and unfamiliar to you. Keep my card, please. Call if you need anything or if you have other questions."

As I stood there numb to the core with tears running down my face, I tried to thank the officer for her help and patience. She walked up to me and gave me a sincere hug before gathering her things to leave. Later when my thoughts were clearer, I was disappointed in myself for the resentful feelings I had toward this woman before even giving her a chance. She took time to explain things I never knew I would need to know or understand.

After the officer left, I walked back into the house for the first time. I was bombarded with the chaotic scene of our kitchen chairs, the table, and a sofa angrily shoved out of place. Sofa cushions and decorative pillows were scattered haphazardly all over the floor. Sterile packaging, tubing, and used syringes were strewn wherever they had been opened. To think I had spent this very morning dusting, sweeping, mopping—or, if Donnie had come in from working and had made a mess such as this, I would have had plenty to say! Now, oddly for me, I didn't care. I had a much more important situation to face.

Our three adult children and their families would soon be arriving from their scattered Texas locations to celebrate the much-anticipated Paw Patrol birthday party. Giving in to my overwhelming sadness, I collapsed on the sofa tearfully trying to imagine how I would ever be able to tell them about the disaster which took place as they looked forward to a weekend of celebration.

As the afternoon became quiet and darkness settled over the day like a blanket, one by one, the kids began to arrive. In the few minutes it took for them to reach our lake house, I prayed, *God, give me the strength to tell my kids why their daddy is not here. Please walk with me through this nightmare.*

I was thankful for the special time I had with each child upon their arrival. This made it possible for me to share the devastating news tailored to each of their situations and personalities. Upon each arrival, I would receive a tired, but happy call announcing, "We're here!" signaling me to remotely open the entry gate.

After opening the gate, I made sure I was outside to greet them.

Clint and his family were the first to arrive after a long day of traveling from Lubbock, Texas.

"Hey, Mom, we finally made it!"

"Oh, I know you guys must be so tired!"

"We are, but we're glad to finally be here!"

"I'm opening the gate for you."

I repeated my prayer for the strength I would need as I headed out to the driveway. The birthday boy was freed from his car seat and jumped out of the car while Mom and Dad stretched their legs and hugged me. While hugging my son, I started to cry.

"Hey Mom, what's wrong?"

Struggling to pull myself together, I told him the story as best as I could. It was excruciating to tell him that his father had passed away that afternoon.

"No, he didn't! You're lying!"

"I know you're shocked and upset. You know I would never lie to you about something this serious."

Tearfully, he grabbed his young son and walked off into the woods behind our lake house.

The pain of telling this child such devastating news was indescribable. I was fully aware I would be repeating this excruciating conversation two more times before the day's end.

Before long, the phone rang again with our second son, Chris, arriving.

"Hi, Mom! I'm here at the gate."

"Okay, I'm happy you got here safely. I'm opening the gate for you." I repeated my prayer for ability, strength, and wisdom for the right words and went outside. After he parked the truck, he jumped out, we hugged each other, and I took a deep breath.

"I have something I need to tell you."

"What?"

I relayed the story to him with a few different but accurate details. During the time I was trying so desperately to tell him the details of the incident, all I saw in his face was complete, genuine sadness. As I tried to talk, this sensitive young man just stared at me with tears flowing down his face. No words, just tears. This image is forever seared into my memory.

"Dad's heart was never able to beat regularly on its own. He passed away late this afternoon." All we could do was fall into the comfort of each other's embrace and cry. My sister and brother-in-law walked over from their lake house joining in our grief and offering us their support.

Finally, our daughter and grandson arrived after a long day of work and travel from Houston. With the gate opened, we all walked outside together knowing what had to be said. Her uncle met her at her car and opened the door to help her out. After a full round of hugs, kisses, and words of welcome, she asked, "Where's Daddy?"

I just stood there searching for the words I didn't want to deliver. Tears clouded my eyes.

"What's wrong? Mommy I'm scared! What's wrong?"

"Earlier today Daddy and I were trying to hang the trampoline swing. There was an accident when the ladder twisted while Daddy was trying to nail a board to the tree. When the ladder twisted, Daddy fell off the ladder."

With desperation in her voice, she asked again. "Mom, where is Daddy?"

"Sweetheart, he passed away late this afternoon."

"What?? No, I don't believe you! How could this happen?" She was inconsolable. We were all there to soothe and support her, except for the one person she needed the most, her daddy.

The reactions to the loss of one of the most important people in my children's young lives were all unique. I want to believe I handled each unique situation with love and care. It's difficult, knowing I will never be able to erase the heartbreak I had to deliver to each of them.

Our oldest grandson was also heart-broken by the news. He had been Grumpy's only grandson for fourteen years. The two of them were very close as his paternal grandfather, Opa, had tragically lost his life when our grandson was only eight years old. Grumpy stepped up to continue Opa's legacy providing guidance, modeling leadership, and of course, sharing his love of the outdoors.

Our second grandson, fifteen years younger, was the birthday boy that weekend. The party was planned with all things Paw Patrol. Decorations, brightly wrapped gifts, birthday cake, streamers, and everything in between would be ready to celebrate. It seemed strange to think we would be celebrating the day after we lost Donnie. I just wasn't able to call off the birthday party. I felt it was important to celebrate our grandson on his third birthday. Our hearts were broken, our minds confused, and our bodies exhausted. But a birthday party experienced through the eyes of a child proved to be a brief respite from our suffering.

~~⚬~~

In September of the following year, our family rejoiced with the gift of another beautiful grandson. Sadly, Donnie would not get to share his love with this funny, energetic little boy. I often visualize the fun these two brothers would have experienced with Grumpy! Regrettably our two youngest grandchildren will not experience or come to know the great man he was.

Our three grown children have missed and have needed their dad throughout these past years. Father's Day is always a difficult day now. On this day, we find ourselves remembering the many stories and incidents that remind us why we loved Donnie so much. Not having him here with us is a loss for all who knew and loved him. We are slowly learning to adjust to our new lives, carrying his love and memories in our hearts each day.

Donnie has an identical twin brother. Everything about their physical appearances was identical including their piercing blue eyes. It's painful and confusing for me to see him in person now, as of course, I see Donnie. When I see him, my breath is taken away. Tears immediately form, and I begin to cry. My immediate sensory reaction is relief, but only for a mere second or two before my brain clears and reminds me that this is not Donnie.

The days and months following Donnie's death were a blur. I was lost, scared, lonely, miserable, and unable to care about anything. After the funeral, legal paperwork was attended to, calls and visits from friends continued, thank you notes were written—but my grief remained stronger than ever. I was lonesome and frightened. It was a challenge for me to exist in a world where everyone was functioning normally as if nothing had happened. My family and friends were supportive and present; however, my new reality was crystal clear: I was alone. Everything in my life would now be my sole responsibility. For me, this reality translated to fear. Fear wasted no time establishing a permanent residence in the pit of my stomach. How could I go on without Donnie?

I had two basic responsibilities I knew I had to perform: my dogs had to be fed, and the bills had to be paid. Truthfully, these two tasks were all I could manage. It did not matter to me if the house was clean, if the laundry was done, or if there was food in the refrigerator. In my state of mind, I had no reason to care about any of these things.

Although I didn't worry about basic housekeeping, I was anxious about what to do if something broke and how to fix it. I had lost every bit of confidence I had prior to Donnie's death. He knew how to fix everything; I knew nothing about repairs. How would I know whom to call and, more importantly, to trust? What would I say if I ever had the courage to make the call? What would be a fair price for the repair I needed? The easiest course of action on my part was to ignore the situation and eventually to consult my sons when the situation could no longer be ignored.

Days turned into weeks, and weeks turned into months, and months turned into years...in fact, five years! I don't recall the exact time I began to crawl out of the miserable state my life had become. I clearly remember feeling I could no longer live this dismal, depressed life, but I had no real plan where to begin.

But I was certain of one thing: I would continue raising puppies for Southeastern Guide Dogs, Inc.; I needed them as much as they needed me. In 1994, our family began an amazing journey with this organization. Donnie and I felt we needed to model the act of volunteering to our young children. Our daughter was involved in Girl Scouts, and the boys were active in Boy Scouts. Of course, these scouting organizations promoted volunteering, but as a family we had not become involved in any formal way to give back. In our local newspaper, I read a notice regarding an upcoming meeting for anyone interested in raising young puppies, preparing them to possibly become guide dogs for the blind. We were a dog-loving family, so this volunteer opportunity seemed like a perfect fit for us.

When I attended the meeting, to my surprise, I was the only person there. After submitting our application and successfully completing the approval process, our family was approved to be puppy raisers. Then, our journey began.

When Donnie passed away, we were midway through raising our twenty-second puppy named Dallas. I never entertained the idea of not continuing this life-changing opportunity for those who are visually impaired. Not only were these puppies a lifeline for those with vison loss but working with these dogs had also become one of my core values. There was no time to sit around feeling sorry for myself; the puppies needed to be fed and walked each day. When Donnie died, I felt I had a responsibility to continue what we started those many years ago.

Today, I'm continuing to raise guide dog puppies—clearly one of the best decisions I've ever made. My challenge is to dedicate the time and effort into raising a dog who will make a positive difference in someone's life. There is no reason to weigh myself down with thoughts of "Why me?" when I can be part of a positive change for others. As I write this story, I'm raising our twenty-seventh beautiful puppy, Sloan.

In addition to raising puppies for those less fortunate than myself, after Donnie's passing, I knew I needed to start learning what my identity was without him being by my side. This proved to be a much more difficult task than the work I did with puppies. I began by reading a great book, *Healing After Loss, Daily Meditations for Working Through Grief*, by Martha Whitmore Hickman. Then I re-read this book with a new purpose—to examine myself and then learn how others were able to live peacefully after the loss of a loved one. Reading my Bible and praying daily also helped me recover from my deep loss.

I was committed to my new daily ritual and soon began to feel stronger. As I began to heal, I discovered I could allow myself to remember the many extraordinary occasions and events in our thirty-nine years of marriage. But I continued to allow myself to feel sadness when it surfaced and to cry when the tears came.

Most importantly, I made a promise to myself to say "yes" whenever possible to invitations extended to me, even if I felt uncomfortable or vulnerable. This one self-imposed policy has quite possibly made the most positive impact because I learned how to be comfortable as a single person. As a result of that promise, I have met many people and gained many new friends—people I may have never had the pleasure of knowing. I have traveled with friends on ships and planes to the Caribbean Islands, Las Vegas, New Hampshire, and Florida. Although I was a bit nervous at first, I now feel quite comfortable driving alone to visit family and friends in Lubbock, Houston, Austin, and Waco.

Recently, I was asked if I would consider taking a part-time job. Once again, I reminded myself of my "yes" promise. I agreed to try it, and I currently enjoy facilitating online classes for students enrolled in Richland College's Collegiate Program.

Being part of a new group has been another blessing that has come from meeting interesting people. At the invitation of a friend, I began attending a Sunday School class at my church. I was uncertain at first, thinking I might not fit in. As I look back, I know I made the right decision to walk through that classroom door. Every woman wholeheartedly welcomed me exactly as I was. I still feel loved and supported by each of these wonderful ladies. So many positive, fun opportunities have come my way because I took the chance to join others.

Although I'm proud of my progress as a single person, I continue to have difficulty knowing what to do or whom to call when home repairs are needed. I usually ignore the problem until I muster up enough courage to make the phone call. More times than not, I still have a hard time trusting myself to make decisions. Donnie, on the other hand, was never afraid to decide anything. He gathered the facts, looked at the situation, weighed his options, and made his choice. I was always so impressed with his confidence!

Thankfully, I have become more comfortable attending social events alone. Recently, my high school class celebrated our fiftieth reunion. I delayed my response and narrowly missed the RSVP deadline. But then I reminded myself of my "yes" promise and mailed my response card indicating I would attend all the events. The weekend arrived, and I had many hesitations: What if no one recognized me, or worse, what if I didn't recognize them? What if I had no one to mingle with or take pictures with? Again, I trusted my "yes" pledge. I packed my suitcase, drove to my hometown of Waco, and attended all the events I had signed up for. My fears and hesitations proved to be a waste of energy as I had a fun, memorable time reconnecting with old friends. Saying "yes" has given me the confidence to become an active participant in my own life.

Today, I find myself a much-improved, self-assured woman. As I look in the mirror and view myself now living a single life, I see a happy, well-adjusted woman. I am surprised but pleased with the progress I have made.

Along with the happy days, there are still certainly some tough days. As a result of my personal tragedy, I have developed a stronger set of coping skills. These skills have enabled me to enjoy the exceptional gifts in my life and to better manage the stressful times.

Donnie's death is certainly the most difficult challenge I have ever experienced. I suppose I should feel fortunate; countless others continue to suffer with no perceived end of their suffering in sight. I am determined to keep moving forward.

Our lake house is still one of our children and grandchildren's favorite places to spend time. Our oldest grandson recently brought his girlfriend for a weekend visit. What fun it was to share our "Camelot" with her! Campfires, golf cart rides, walks around the lake, and fishing were on the agenda each day. Recently, the bald eagles returned in all their beauty to share their magnificent flights over the lake.

After that dreadful day, the trampoline swing was packed away with no intention of ever being hung. It continues to reside on the uppermost shelf in a closet, nestled in a non-descript box that no one would ever notice. With each trip to the lake, as I store my suitcase for the weekend, my eyes glance upwards to that box. Our two young grandsons are now four and eight years old. As surprising as it may seem, I have been contemplating the future of the swing. Lately, I've found myself wondering if the swing should come down off the shelf and provide our grandchildren with all the joy Donnie and I were certain it would bring.

Chaos and Silence

Dinah Harris

My mother had me early so she could fit into a dress.

The dress, I was told, was a slinky royal blue number, privately tailored by Milo, the queer designer living across the street in the salmon-pink house with the ugly blue shutters.

"Milo, you know I can't wear that. It's too…old," she gawked.

"Honey, if you can't make it look good, nobody can."

My mother, Joanie Harris, a singer-songwriter (think Dolly Parton crossed with wacko supermodel Janice Dickinson) had a knack for surrounding herself with "yes" people. The need to be yes-ed was part of her whole story. "The Straight Shot Gal" was her chosen moniker because she liked guns and shooting innocent birds from a distance. The NRA often invited her to their "celebrity" shooting events, not because she was famous—despite her thinking everyone's always bugging her for autographs—but because she flirted with rednecks, and my dad made large donations to the NRA.

I grew up rich, spoiled rotten, and raised by a rotating team of nannies to whom I owe my tenacity and compassion. I know, I know.

Poor little rich girl. Being rich doesn't protect you from trauma, but it sometimes makes the trauma easier.

Encounters were brief and centered around whatever my mother wanted to do that day. Peering in on her routines was like theater: watch the woman bounce around to Jane Fonda; admire how quickly she flicks red paint onto her nails; see how she stands on her tippy toes and turns slightly to the side to check that her uterus doesn't make her look fat; fall into her beauty, reflected in the mirror as a preview of your own worth; note how she pinches her skin here and there, above the hip, on the upper arm, the outer thigh, the inner thigh, even the wrists and ankles. Copy/paste every pinch and flaw onto yourself, standing in front of the mirror, learning how to be a person—not just any person, but a real woman—goddess, model, actress, beauty queen, source of envy—everything but a mother.

A mother didn't fit into a size double-zero from the 80s. A mother would never wear tighter clothes than mall rat teens. A mother couldn't possibly flit around in lingerie with her nipples sticking out. And a mother sure as hell didn't crash your parties with friends while wearing a translucent, untied robe with one bulbous boob stealing the show.

"Oh, I know Mrs. Harris," said the boys at school.

Did I know her? This Mrs. Harris seemed to be quite a popular character, very different from the one I'd seen sobbing over a bottle of tequila, wearing a slinky black dress, and stretched across a black backdrop like the anti-mother pinup she'll always be in her head.

Growing up with a country singer for a mother and a father who is best described as a mixture between Jack Nicholson and George Bush,

I could not escape noise. Between her humming, clacking heels, and wannabe country riffs and his booming sneezes, blaring televisions, and barking conference calls, our house was chaos.

The only time I enjoyed the noise was when she'd play the piano. Be it classical or ragtime, I'd dance wild and flailing, then slowing my limbs to a honeyed pace as she altered the tempo just to see what I'd do. But one can only play so much piano, and one can only dance for so long, right? These are the best memories I have of my mother.

As for my father, one of my most vivid memories was of the back of his head crowning over the driver's headrest like a fuzzy hill and the sound of ice cubes rattling in the cupholder as the wheels of the van toyed with the white lines on the side of the road. Almost every other weekend, my sister, mom, dad, and I packed into the big black Ford van and drove three hours east to "The Farm" (AKA grandma's house) in Carthage, Texas.

I'd listen to my Walkman and stare out at the passing trees, wondering if the birds were watching me watch them—odds were, one of them had to be, even if by accident. My dad didn't allow the radio on in the car for the most part, but when music was present, it was something like "Now That's the 60s!" or Elvis' Christmas album, no matter the time of year. My mom still hummed over whatever was playing; hence, my Walkman was crucial to drown out the clashing sounds, or if the music was turned off, as it was 90% of the time, the cold silence.

The only thing I really had to watch out for was the inimitable shake of a Styrofoam cup. When that happened, Stef and I sprang into action: ¾ ice, ¼ Maker's Mark, a splash of Coca Cola, and ½-inch left at the top. I was a backseat bartender from the time I was strong enough to fish a can out of the icebox.

At the time, I didn't realize drinking and driving was a bad thing. To me, it was normal to see the Styrofoam cup in one hand, the other hand resting against the bottom-right sliver of the wheel. I admired the way he didn't fully grasp the wheel; he just rested his hand against it like you would test whether the kettle's hot.

The coolest part of those drives was toward the end when he'd let me or Stef sit on his lap and steer the van along the narrow country road that oscillated between pavement, gravel, and dirt. Feeling in control of such a large, heavy vehicle while on the lap of a man whose full attention I desperately craved felt powerful and safe.

~~~

Waking to the whistle of a kettle, I remember the farm being a place where time had a habit of slowing down. Perhaps it was the rolling pasture and the endless Texas pines stretching so high that if you hiked deep enough into the woods, you couldn't see the sky; or maybe it was the little white house, still boasting pots, pans, and cabinets from the early 20th century. This was where my paternal grandmother, Mabelle, ran the show. She was eighty-four when I was ten years old and, like me, routine was her thing.

Every morning, just after five o'clock, I'd hear her remove the kettle from the front burner on the stove, turn the gas off, and fuss with the coffee can. Then there would be a pause followed by the sound of a lid popping off an aluminum tin and then the blip of something plopping into her mug. A chocolate-covered cherry in her coffee was a hell of a greeting to the day.

"Just a dollop of tequila in her coffee every morning!" my dad and Uncle Rich would say. I was never sure if she actually did it or if they were saying she did to convince us and themselves that drinking tequila in their coffee was a normal way to wake up.

I was too young to ever grow close to my grandmother, but I recall her being someone who saw me and seemed to benefit from my presence. In the morning, we'd walk through the garden plucking cherry tomatoes right off the vine and popping them in our mouths. One time I recall her whipping a saltshaker out of her apron pocket for us to season them right there.

During the extreme summer heat, we'd plant ourselves on the white, shaded porch swing and snap green beans, ends in one pail, centers in another. I'm sure she probably told me stories of some kind, but I remember the silence the most. She had a keen reverence for silence, but it was different than the silence of the car ride; this was a still, plush kind of silence—not a sour, tight silence. At eight years old, I wondered if she was also dreaming up names of colors and undiscovered birds; at thirteen, I imagined how embarrassing it must've been for her to wear one of those huge menstruation contraptions in the 20s; at seventeen, I wondered if she'd live long enough to see me on TV, her magic portal to Billy Graham, which she blasted any time my dad and uncle weren't watching football. Evangelical folly aside, she was sharp, especially for the fact that she was the one adult who didn't take my mother's BS.

"Now, Joanie, that's downright silly," she'd scold her. As a kid, I was fascinated by the drama my mother created—on one end, people idolized her and treated her like a goddess (partly because she demanded that of them, partly because she was quite an interesting character), on the other, she really had a knack for pissing people off. The pissed-off cohorts, I eventually realized, were the ones I really cared about—the ones who lived in reality, not in Joanie's special version of it.

The lobby of the Embassy Suites was at full capacity for Fan Fair, the quintessential country music festival in Nashville. She'd been signing autographs and taking pictures with adoring fans all day. Most had never heard of "The Straight Shot Gal," but there were a few podunk rednecks who seemed honored to be in her presence. Especially middle-aged or older, married or recently divorced men who always held her too close for photo ops.

Despite my punk-preteen sass and my hatred for country music, I was proud to be the daughter of such a beautiful woman with whom everybody seemed to fall in love. And it made me happy to see her smile in her element of being adored. Even if she later bitched about all the "creepy" men with their "fat-ass wives."

The hotel room was cramped with boxes of merchandise, CDs, and three suitcases of her outfits and shoes. Yellow, stale light made the room all the more depressing. She was already mid-way through a bottle of Don Julio tequila. Her eyeshadow creased with oil, and her fake lashes recoiled from her eyelids.

"I just don't know what to do next—it's just not good—I can't do this anymore—you think I'm good? My music?" She poured two shots of tequila, pushing the latter toward me on the coffee table.

Who was this dribbling mess of a woman?

"Well, you can write," I replied with as much confidence as a tween can summon. "You can play any instrument that's put in front of you." I summoned up the best solid adult voice I could muster.

"I'm proud of you, Mommy." *Was I? Was I convincing enough?* I downed the shot before retrieving tissues from the bathroom.

Despite my dad's alcoholism, he and I always shared a secret language: mom's crazy. Whenever they fought, Stef and I assumed our roles as henchmen. She and my mom, me and my dad. I suppose we split that way because I was always told I took after him. My earliest baby photos reveal the same no-BS furrow and cleft chin. I was a cute, angry, bulldog of a child. We also reacted similarly to conflict: stay quiet, sneaky, and small. Let the other party tucker themselves out before you strike. Then use your words—the nastiest ones, if appropriate.

"If she had a brain, she'd take it out and play with it," he regularly complained to me of my mother. And I agreed—even laughed because it was a funny, morbid mental image. Plus, I had no idea how to recognize verbal or emotional abuse.

The emphasis on insulting her intelligence also made it all the more powerful when he looked at my report card and said he was proud of me. In a way, I felt like the backup wife, the one who could make up for my mother's lack of brains and corroborate when he was obviously right—which was 99.9% of the time. Later, my psychologist would refer to this as "emotional incest."

When they weren't bickering, both he and my mother would pit Stef and me against each other. They'd pay me to tattle and spy on her and laugh when she inevitably laid into me with slaps, pushes, and even attempted strangulation, which was rare, but it happened. He would shower me with compliments in front of Stef, often in direct rebuttal of some accomplishment she had gushed about in dire need of approval. My mom would brag on and on about Stef's long legs and golden hair.

Being his favorite was wonderful, don't get me wrong, but it cost me my sisterhood. To this day, my sister treats everything like a competition. My dad tore her down so much that she feels she has a right to tear me down at every opportunity; thus, I forfeited the role of sister. Sometimes it's easier to lose a piece of your identity than to change someone.

Thankfully, school was the opposite of home as I finally had a place to succeed and be validated. I attended an elite private school throughout middle and high school, a school filled with brick-thick textbooks and a twisted idea of God. Despite its colorful stained-glass windows, the chapel looked like it was modeled after a looney bin—white naked walls with twisted beams supporting a triangular steeple toward the front. If you squinted just right, the beams could mirror holy lobotomy contraptions.

Amid typical private school tomfoolery, I forged a separate identity for myself—the ultimate people pleaser with just enough spice to win ever-prized attention and affirmation. I was fortunate to have some great teachers and got used to the perfectionistic high of straight-A's. I loved proving my peers—mainly boys—wrong when they thought I was a pretty idiot.

The first time I was raped was at a Hilton Garden Inn somewhere in Kansas. I was twelve years old. My maternal grandparents, Alfred

and Edith, were celebrating their fortieth anniversary by renewing
their wedding vows at a pancake house.

The lobby of the hotel was tall and open.

"Where y'all from?" The boys had Midwestern accents and had
traded their military fatigues for swim trunks.

"Dallas."

"City girls."

While my sister approached fearlessly, I hid next to a fake peace
plant with Styrofoam for soil. Eventually, I plopped into the hot tub.
They had beer, so we had beer. I was almost thirteen and, when tipsy,
felt proud of my sprouting boobs.

Jake, John, or something with a J…Whatever his name, J had that
effortless bad boy hotness to him. The lines on his forehead signaled
he was almost thirty. After hot tubbing for a few hours and retiring to
the boys' room for beer and cigarettes, J insisted on walking me back to
my room "like a gentleman," he said. We took the stairs because "we'll
have more time to talk." I remember thinking how sweet that was.

I was barely five-feet tall at the time, and he was probably closer
to six feet, so he did that Hollywood thing where he lifted me up and
forced me to straddle him against the wall in the stairwell. He pushed
into my lips so forcefully, his stubble burned my face. His tongue almost made it all the way down my shallow throat a few times.

One of his hands clutched and kneaded my boobs like he was trying to push me away, but his other hand pushed me towards him. I
was squeezed in place. His hips started to thrust under me, and I felt
his belt buckle scrape against my pubic bone a few times, which hurt,
but I couldn't stop thinking of how sexy this must look, so I ignored

it. Then he dropped me, unbuckled his belt, inched his pants down, and grabbed my shoulders, lowering me to my knees with my face at his crotch.

"Nonono," I whispered. At least I think I did. My mouth burdened by him, it may have sounded like a nasally "mmmnnnnmmnooo" sound.

I tried to push him away, but he was stronger, his hands and body urgent about the matter.

So began the string of sexual abuses.

The floor of a movie theater in seventh grade. A friend's lake house in eighth grade. A boy's attached garage party room in ninth and tenth grade. The back bed of a pickup, the roof and back seat of a car. The pool house bathroom on my sixteenth birthday. All the times and places I distinctly remember saying no and wasn't heard.

Half the other times, I didn't say no. I hated my body. Fuck it. Let 'em have it.

~ ~

The Hollywood Juice Diet involved drinking nothing but sugar water with Red 40, ginger, and probably some laxative disguised as "rejuvenating" for two days. This was my mommy-and-me bonding material in fifth through seventh grade.

We'd also get up at 5:30 am and jog a 3.5-mile path around the neighborhood. I forget what we talked about, but I'm assuming we probably covered the best exercises for thin thighs (*Thin Thighs in 30*

Days! was a prized VHS tape she and I passed back and forth), which celebrities looked fat, marketing ploys for her next album, and who of my or Stef's friends' moms had "work" done. But it couldn't have all been gossip or garbage. Sometimes we rescued actual garbage, an act that was probably wrapped up in her hoarding tendencies and contributed to my current love of second-hand goods.

One of my favorite rescued paintings has hung in my bedroom since middle school: an oil painting of two wild horses, one black, one auburn. The eye of the auburn horse is the focal point, a vortex of oily onyx, while the more poised black horse looks on just behind the other, nurturing, regal, and wild.

⟞⟝

Jerry was a personal trainer at the YMCA in a ritzy-racist borough of Dallas, just a ten-minute drive from home. My sister and my mom had gone there for years. And, apparently, I went there as a tot for karate.

Jerry was twenty-six, and I was a fifteen-year-old exercise addict. I wanted toned volleyball-goddess arms. I wanted surfboard abs. Long legs. Tits. Blonde. I wanted to be anything remotely lovable.

He had Nordic white-blonde hair, ghostly white shrimp-pink skin, and a lean stature with muscly bulges paired with a hockey player's nose, skinny bowlegs, and piercing blue eyes. He was a wannabe punk with a stellar sense of humor and a smartass disposition.

He'd perch on the windowsill in front of the treadmill, and we'd talk about music, SouthPark, politics, or my mother. He'd seen her come in many times in prior years and couldn't help but notice her laughably bulbous fake tits and Crayola tan. In retrospect, he helped me compartmentalize her as the lunatic that she was so that I could get on with my life as normally as possible.

In our relationship, I played the young, innocent, attractive ingenue, and he played the older male savior, the daddy who might save me—or at the very least distract me—from feelings of isolation and unworthiness. The logic at the time: older men who want me are more valuable because they could have anyone. But look, here's one choosing me. Like my mother, I had no clue what I was doing.

Of course, Jerry did. He chose me for a reason that had nothing to do with me.

The first time he kissed me, he whispered, "You're not that young in your head, you know?"

"Thanks, I guess...You're not that old in your head, either."

Young and old—yin and yang. We seemed to fit in a way that no one would understand. And, in my head, that made it special.

I blew off my high school friends who sparked his jealousy and ire for "taking all my time." I slept over on school nights. One morning at his place, I had put on my school uniform: a white button-down with a green plaid pleated skirt, high socks, and saddle oxfords.

"I want to say...this is sexy...," he said. There was an unspoken "but" there. And in the back of my head, I knew why the "but" was there. But I'm in fucking high school. But I'm basically a child, and you're a full-grown man pushing thirty. A man eleven years older than me. A man who waited for me to become the "legal" age of seventeen to have sex with me so he wouldn't get charged with statutory rape— even when he damn well should. Deep in the part of my brain where I store all the painful things, I knew I was complicit.

"I'm in love with Jerry," I confessed to my mother. Tears came, and I figured it was because of something like honesty.

My mother laughed.

If I could zip back into that moment, I'd stomp into the room, slap her across the face, and scream: "Hello! I'm in love with someone who is close to being a sexual predator and a statutory rapist! What the hell is wrong with you? What the hell is wrong with me?!?!"

"I'm proud of you, honey." Her tone was half perfunctory, half encouraging.

I sobbed. She chuckled and practiced her Farrah Fawcett hair flip.

After a few bellows, I laughed. I recall feeling relieved. How dumb to be crying so hard over admitting that I had a boyfriend.

Deep down, my body was probably having a visceral response to the dark shame I felt and the fact that I had no idea what to do with the scene that had just unfolded. My mother telling me she's proud of my "dating" a loser who preys on high school girls.

You go and spill your big sob story, and nobody hears you. Your voice is—you are—worthless.

～〜〜

At UCLA, I tried my best to disappear. Mostly silent and devastatingly bitter, I purposely carried myself like a vampire so that people would stay away from me. I held everything in; the chaos and anger percolated in me until I became a depressive, semi-paranoid recluse. The only time I let it out was in acting classes; not claiming the anger as my own made it safe. But once classes were over, the walls rose around me again, etched with enough haunted memories, anxieties, and what-ifs that I had to distract myself with food—and the lack thereof—and exercise to avoid being vulnerable to them. Peace and rest were vulnerable states I couldn't allow.

I'd have intense debates with an inner self I named Justine, a voice that seemed hell-bent on destroying me: *What if you peeled your skin with a cheese grater, or better, that big Santoku knife? Would a ten-story drop really kill you or just break your legs? Who will take care of your cats when your body is found? Who would care?*

Justine, a mixture of my eating disorder voice and this new voice was my sick little distraction from the fact that I had no control over the world around me. But what was "me" anyway? Me was a vessel of Prozac, Abilify, bi-weekly psychologist appointments, binge-purge sessions, blackout drunk nights, and smoking weed to nurse the aftermath. Eat, sleep, study, drink, eat, puke, smoke, repeat. A sharp, yet empty little girl who wanted everyone to like her but was too terrified and disgusted to make an effort to reach out. My sickest thought whispered: slow suicide.

~⌇~

After graduating in 2011, I felt a boost of confidence. Amid the depression of the last four years, I'd already managed to be in a couple of films, music videos, and television productions. Unconsciously,

I was doing exactly what my mother would want, despite not having seen her more than once a year.

Los Angeles presented all the tools of chaos I needed: the entertainment industry of monkeys, a saturation of various drugs, and shady characters with whom to do the drugs.

I started working at an Indian gastropub, and I got my blow and ketamine from a short little dishwasher from El Salvador named Papi. So went a typical Tuesday night at work, the most reliable structure afforded to me: drop chicken-tikka poutine at table three, go behind the bar for a bump, take tamarind chutney to table seven, duck behind the restocking station for a swig of vodka, greet customers at table two, take a bump, enter more naan bread for table seven, and so on until I could snort and sip without distraction.

At the end of most nights, all the cash I earned went up my nose or down my throat. Through all this, my dad was, for some reason, still sending me money. I remember he asked me one day if I was on drugs. I can't remember what I told him.

The motivation to get up and do anything was geared toward getting drunk or high. I'd lost weight to the degree that my belts didn't work, and I burned triangular patterns into my arms and thighs because it felt good. I called it art. I was chaos.

You know the old saying, "Don't throw money at a problem?" That was the opposite of what my dad did. By my mid-twenties, I'd pissed away all the money he threw at me over the years. For him, money was love; it was a key factor of his identity, as though he lived to earn it and protect his daughters from his childhood lack of money, which made the whole endeavor seem too noble to resent. My rampant spending (mostly on things that all hurt me) was a passive-aggressive way of rejecting him; then again, addiction is an amorphous, crazy thing. So, I pissed away all but a very important sliver. And in a world where money makes certain things easier, that sliver saved me.

I spent it on therapy and meditation retreats and crafts that fed my soul like painting, music, and reading. Where his emotional capacity to validate and truly see me failed, his money stepped in. In a way, I think he knew his shortcomings, hence his great generosity—a level of generosity you typically don't see from hyper-capitalist, pre-Trump Republican, depression-era babies. What he couldn't invest in me emotionally, I invested in myself monetarily. For that gift, I feel indebted to him. Maybe that explained his generosity—he knew he'd always be needed as "The Provider."

～～

"DD, it's Mumu—your mother! I'm here. Outside your door!"

My mother was, in fact, calling me from outside my apartment door. I was frozen on the other side, watching through the peephole. She was in town for a supposed "songwriters' meeting."

Her skin was an orange spray tan, and she wore spaghetti straps and a bra top, her boulder tits and bullet nipples shooting out like threats because she should have listened to her surgeon and gone with a C-cup instead. And I can guess she was wearing heels—always—despite having talon toes like the mangled curly fries she'd scarf down and puke up.

"Jack Nicholson's still on board!" This was pure hogwash, her girlish dreams of stardom—she said things like this a lot. Like when I received texts at 4 a.m. saying that she was hand-delivering her famous meatloaf to the White House for Trump.

"I have a package for you but don't want to leave it out here—confidential, you know—my new singles and some knick-knacks."

For every holiday, she sent me at least twenty of her CDs, both old and new. I still have no idea how she paid for them considering, by that point, she'd probably spent her multi-million-dollar divorce settlement on luxury getaways to Switzerland and elsewhere to score cheaper prescription drugs, since all the local pharmacies knew to turn her away.

Usually, the new CDs were different combinations of old, recycled songs she recorded ten years ago but with photos of her newly reconstructed face, tits, lips, or cheeks. Her repurposed plastic identity.

"Hope to see you, little one! You are my daughter. I am your mother." Biological fact. Who was she trying to convince? Herself?

"I think I deserve to see you every so often." Deserve? As if I'm property she bought twenty-eight years ago. Her voice started to crack like it always does when she's going to cry.

"Hate to cry, but you know me…" Oh, I know. She always got to cry more than I did. I was the mom; she was the child.

～～

"I'm not ready," I told Jennifer, my psychologist, when she brought up in-patient treatment.

"I ate a sandwich," I lied to Erin, my nutritionist, who causally munched on oranges and nuts throughout our session as a lowkey way of normalizing snacks.

I had been heavily into Buddhism at the time and had studied it off and on since going off to college. I even shaved my head, which caused some alarm among my mental-health team.

"Dinah," Jennifer only ever said my name when she was about to ask a biggie. "If I could reach into your head with a pencil and just erase your eating disorder entirely, would you like that?"

"Hell, yes!"

"Would you really?" She raised her hand like a stop sign, what she called a "sacred pause." The gesture signaled me to check in, close my eyes, and feel my internal, conscious eye drop into the space below my navel. I'd let it rest there for a few breaths until it came back to my brain with a message.

"Well, I dunno," I admitted. *Who would I be without my trauma, my story, my rules?*

"Why not?" She cocked her head and leaned in. "What would you miss?"

She had me do a writing assignment about all the things the eating disorder gave me.

My internal voice was strong. It was measurable and dependable. It gave me rules to follow and quantitative statistics to measure my progress.

"It was a tool," I said during the next session, paraphrasing from my journal. "It allowed me to survive for almost a decade in that house and after."

"Right! It was very good for that purpose, wasn't it?"

"I guess, but it's not really good now... it's kinda, outdated..."

"So, Dinah," there it was again. "What would it take for you to be able to say to your eating disorder: Thank you for keeping me alive, but you can go now."

～∾～

The Bella Mente was a swanky eating disorder recovery home.

All my stuff was taken, and I could hear it being rifled through but couldn't see which items were being stolen, tossed, or sorted. I wondered if they'd jack my baby ring, the only physical object that still connected me to my family and the idea that someone may have cared about me in the outside world.

A woman in a chic matching outfit sat me down on a red IKEA loveseat and crossed her legs, dangling a low, blocky heel in front of the glass coffee table, manicured with fake stargazer lilies and spiritual growth magazines. She asked me why I was there.

"Because I'm tired of being sick."

"Sick? How so?" She was baiting me. *Don't trust her*, I told myself. I crossed my legs in the opposite direction and bounced a foot.

"Shouldn't you know?"

She cleared her throat, blinked at me, then lowered her gaze.

"I can't love," I spoke the words as if reading the name of an album, each word capitalized. I shifted to cross my legs at my ankles, all demure. Act weak.

"Love?" she repeated, the same plain tone I used. "You're here be-

160

cause you can't love who?"

I wanted to correct her "who" to "whom" but didn't because she wouldn't learn anyway. I was just another wacko who checked herself into a swanky rehab center in Carlsbad because I didn't know what else to do. But I knew I was sick and tired of my sick and tired life.

"Anyone," I say, which was the truth.

She lifted her chin with a slight purse of the lips and wrote a line of words on the yellow pad on her lap. Who still uses yellow pads? For what I'm paying, they should be able to afford more than a few iPads.

"What about you? Would you say you're incapable of loving yourself?"

I nodded and stared at the furry tendrils shooting out from the center of the lilies. I couldn't remember if that was called the pistil or stamen.

"Love and abuse look a lot alike to me. Bad parents and all that, you know." I half-smiled at my own bitterness. I wished Jennifer was there.

"Well, now that's something we can work on."

"What?" *My parents?*

"Self-love." Right.

"Oh." Starvation brought clarity, and I chewed on that clarity like a rotten tooth.

"Do you want to be here?"

"I checked myself in," I said. "I'm paying a shit ton of money to be here." (My father was paying a shit ton of money for me to be there. I had to get well for his sake.)

She showed me to my room, and I noticed a copy of *The Little*

Prince on the wicker bed stand. My bed felt like the hood of a car, and the bathroom door bore two locks and a keypad.

I shared my room with another girl, Summer, who had the personality of a sock. My fellow patients seemed like people I'd meet in the checkout line at Trader Joe's. Except for Mina, who was set up with a feeding tube in the living room so she could be under 24/7 surveillance while coming down from heroin. In a sick way, I felt better knowing I wasn't a lost cause like she was.

My nurse reminded me of a particularly special nanny who raised me and made the best cornbread I'd ever eaten. She smelled like cinnamon and orange peels, and her voice made me think of the sonorous underbelly of a whale.

I couldn't poop for the first nine days. On day ten, I dropped a few bunny balls worth of crap. The nurse took a peek and wrote a "Y" next to my name on the chart tacked to the wall for all to see.

I smoked a cigarette every time they offered a break, which was every hour. I ranted with the girls about how much the food sucked and listened to how Natalie, with her husky-blue eyes and PJ Harvey lips, had been to sixteen different rehab centers and "knows her patient rights."

On the rare occasions I met with my assigned therapist, she did nothing but nod.

My guitar was missing a string because the fat one on the bottom might be used for self-strangulation.

My armpit hair was now longer than my actual hair because I didn't have razor privileges and didn't care to ask anybody about getting them.

When I finally got an outing "privilege" to leave the house to eat the agreed-upon snack, I devised a plan. As discussed with my psychologist and nutritionist, I was going to get a grande soy cappuccino and a cake pop. They gave me the exact amount of cash I needed from my wallet, and I was to bring the receipt back as proof. I got an Americano, and when the barista turned away, I snagged a ten-pack of instant coffee sachets to sneak back in my panties. When I got back, they searched me first thing. After I was cleared, I shifted my leg and a sachet fell out of my crotch. Damn. I later joked to the others that I'd be a shoddy drug mule.

By day fifteen, I journaled about how I had to hold on because my fake psychologist nodded her head with that look that said: "You poor, sick child. You'd kill yourself if it weren't for this place." I tried to convince myself I needed this place.

On day seventeen, I checked myself out against the advice of my "team." I put *The Little Prince* into my bag, wrapped up in the jeans I never wore because I was swollen with water weight that only sweatpants could mask.

I said goodbye to the girls, even the annoying newbie who had a split tongue like a snake. Sam slipped me a note that said she loved me, and she'd see me on the outside. Natalie looked me in the eye, and I nodded per our agreement to toss some extra strength Nyquil over the back fence for her to fetch and get drunk off of during the last cigarette of the day. My psychologist patted me on the shoulder and said, "You'll do just fine; it was a pleasure," and I knew her naive hope was standard procedure.

Later that day, I got stoned on the beach and plotted to drive to the nearest pizza restaurant, choke down the whole thing, and get rid of it as proof of my agency. I made a mental note to read *The Little Prince*, but I never did. It's a kid's book; I wasn't a kid anymore.

~

For the better part of a decade, I worked with a team of psychologists to mourn the loss of the mother I never had, the mother I wanted, the mother I needed to see me, want me, and need me.

One session, Jennifer had me bring in an old photo of my mother taken when I was a baby. In it, she is sunlight in a blue dress. Her hair is toasted hay falling onto her shoulders, strong and statuesque, framing her décolletage and natural breasts. Her smile is an easy breeze, and her eyes are in full bloom. I can understand why my dad fell in love with her.

I slapped the photo on the table in front of me. Jennifer crooked her head.

"Wow, she's lovely."

"Yup, she was. Before the crazy."

"Oh!" That look of faux surprise she always did, followed by a smile. "You don't say. Well, I never! I had no idea!" She spoke my language of sarcasm and bitterness and enjoyed laughing at my ridiculous insults and ways of repainting the past in such colorful terms. I used humor as a shield as not to run the risk of pity parties.

"Who is this woman? Tell me about her."

"She's an addict, a bitch, a bad mother, a crappy musician… I could go on." Being the daughter of a bad mother—a voluntary half-orphan —was a key piece of my persona.

"But this woman?" she pointed to the picture.

I get it. The mother I had was not the mother in this photo.

"This woman turned into her. She's not drunk or high or throwing things or yelling. She's just there, enjoying being outside."

"And did she ever enjoy being outside with you?"

The only times I recall being outside I was by myself playing in puddles or later running away to camp out at the nearest park for a few hours until she passed out or finished destroying the kitchen during one of her usual binge-and-purge episodes. "I remember being outside but not with her."

"Be outside with her now," she lifted the photo next to her kind, Germanic-round face. "Here, with her here." She put her free hand over her heart.

I tried, but it felt too dumb, too distant.

Years later, it would click that she was inspiring me to become my own mother. To spin a version of her that could replace the story I'd clung to for so long: the one that painted me as the poor victim of an abusive addict.

Since my voice wasn't strong enough yet, Jennifer's voice eventually took the place of my mother's. I discovered I could speak to myself with the same relaxed, accepting tone. What Jennifer didn't know was that I was doing drugs and often showed up high. Oddly, I feel like those times we did psychotherapy while I was stoned or hyped up still made a major impact. In a way, it was me proving to myself that I could be accepted no matter what state I was in. After a few times, she called me on it, and we made an agreement—only sober Dinah came through that door.

～

When I tell people I've overdosed twice, I feel like I'm exaggerating. I know I came pretty close, though. The first time was less of an overdose risk and more of an I'm-leaning-on-a-dude-at-a-bar-because-I-took-too-many-key-bumps-of-ketamine kind of thing. The second overdose started with a Caesar salad I got rid of in the restaurant bathroom and a glass of wine for dinner.

The evening progressed like any other weekday evening with my making the same mistakes and looking just as stupid with the same set of bartenders, addicts, and fellow degenerates.

Two drinks and x-number of lines and key bumps in, I felt alive again. We danced, chain smoked, traded philosophies to feel simultaneously more and less hopeless, and played pool and Pac-Man. We were children again on a playground full of rancid tools.

We took the party back to my place, as usual, because I had paint, a turntable, and a coke table. Once the sun perked up and turned the sky my favorite steely blue, I went to piss. I looked gray, and my eyeballs were 4-D. It was a task to focus on my own reflection, and once I locked eyes with myself, I felt a bottomless sense of fear and sadness. Then, I was numb.

You're an effing rockstar. You make your friends so happy! You are literally at the top of the world.

All these twisted affirmations told me to get back out there, take another bump, and enjoy the present moment. How Buddhist.

I squatted on the toilet, then remembered to stand up again and yank my pants down. After a haphazard wipe, I stood up and felt piss still dripping. I had tried to pull my pants back up but only got them above my knees. My shirt hit below my crotch, so who needed pants anyway?

I waddled out into the living room to find Joel and his friend staring at me.

"You good?"

"Yeah," I chirped. And with that, I felt the room tilt backward at least forty-five degrees. The stool in front of me got sucked into the air until it made contact with my chin. As soon as that happened, the fantasy of reverse gravity faded, and I realized I was falling forward. Then I realized my chin was cold and bleeding. I was on the floor.

I don't remember the immediate reaction of Joel and his buddy, but I suspect it was something like, "Oops…Time to go."

I laid down in bed and felt Joel's body heat next to me for a minute. When I woke up, he was gone. I smoked a bowl to get normal again. An undated journal entry from July 2013 reads: *Too much blow, oopsies.*

The last time I hugged my mother I was at LAX at approximately 10:35 p.m. in October of 2013. I was super drunk, having just deplaned from an eight-hour flight from Honolulu.

Her tits felt hard on my relatively flat chest. I had given up bras at age nineteen; meanwhile, her bullet nipples were still bullets—several botched boob jobs meant her tits would probably survive the nuclear apocalypse.

Her arms didn't so much squeeze as they did envelop, and her forearms delivered two courtesy pats like I needed to be burped. "I'm the mother, and you're the daughter," she always said when she felt like manipulating me. Her hands were doing God knows what behind my back.

That trip, I released my dead cat's ashes into the ocean on a palm leaf and sang "It's All Over Now, Baby Blue," by Bob Dylan.

That trip, I packed cocaine and weed into bottles of bubble bath, which I wrapped in glittery *Congratulations!* wrap and tied with ribbons. TSA wouldn't mess with gifts—they'd feel bad.

That trip, I turned twenty-five. I was so out of it that I only remember half-images. My mother sent bottles of champagne to my room, which, per my request, was located in a different wing of the hotel. We had dinner one night. The other five nights, she never showed. She didn't answer the phone or text except for two times when she said she was "walking out the door" and "almost ready."

I'd never been stood up before. Maybe it was my freshly-shaved head; maybe she was embarrassed by my andro style.

That trip, while waiting at a sushi restaurant, starving and sucking on edamame pods, I watched a family of four eat and laugh. A twelve-year-old girl wore a dress more suited for an orphan. I wrote a poem about a Hawaiian orphan who chose the ocean as her mother.

That trip, I hooked up with one of the bartenders who worked at the hotel pool bar. She was probably around forty and had a tattoo of a deer skull on her chest. We swam naked first and exited the water right before a storm.

That trip, at the hotel pool bar, my mother showed me off to the seventeen-year-old boys she had wooed with alcohol and tits. I took key bumps under a beach towel.

On the plane back to the mainland, my mother flirted with a standard-edition bald, white baby across the aisle and told me I should, too. I watched *Shallow Hal* twice and nodded at every flight attendant who wafted by with a question on their lips and a bottle in tow.

The last time I hugged my mother, it was the hug you give at the end of a one-night stand before they gingerly close the door on your drunk-stoned-strung-out ass, not too fast or too slow.

My mother sent me a book a year later—*How to Forgive When You Don't Feel Like it*. It was a whole slew of Bible verses and comments by TV priests, pastors, and other religious nuts who probably do it for the attention and the tax break. She'd signed the title page: "I forgive YOU. Joanie Harris" in that same decades-old signature I've seen a million times on CDs and posters.

But she's never said she's sorry for anything. Not once—except in the form of "I'm sorry YOU feel that way," a typical narcissistic line that deflects blame back onto the other person. I've apologized hundreds of times for this and that. Even the "please stop texting me" texts. All of it.

I'm not sure I know what I want her to apologize for. It's not like she gave me her eating disorder and addiction in a tidy little box; studies show both have genetic elements, so who's to say she didn't inherit them, too? *Do we get to create our own narratives, or are we characters in stories spanning generations?*

~⌖~

When I moved to Austin in December of 2013, I reinvented my story. I was no longer the actor; I now was someone who could help people. Someone who did good things with my intellect and energy.

I wrote page after page of agreements with myself, something Jennifer taught me to do. I set boundaries with myself and extended them outward.

I was hired at a local charter school to work with elementary students after school. The voice I'd inherited from Jennifer—the mothering voice—mixed with my own verbally spoken voice in ways I didn't expect. I could be gentle with the kids and with myself; I didn't have to be a jaded badass 24/7.

Seeing kids struggle with parents who were struggling themselves was a regular occurrence. It made my connections with them all the more important; it made my voice with them that much more powerful.

I decided to go back to school for a master's degree in humanities and liberal arts with a special focus on creative writing. Drafting stories about myself and others was therapeutic at times, retraumatizing at others. No matter the effect, witnessing myself being courageous on the page showed me that my voice matters.

I also turned my focus back to the Bodhisattva precepts and incorporated those compassion-and-mindfulness-based ideas into literary analysis and analysis of my own past. In a sense, my graduate school education allowed me to relearn how to see the world and interpret stories with a more gentle, authentic, and curious lens.

Being back in the same state as my family of origin presented a plethora of opportunities to set boundaries. I stopped going home for holidays, and when I did go home, I kept the visits brief. I cut off my mother entirely.

"But she's your mother."

"Thou shalt honor thy mother and father."

"She won't live forever."

"You'll regret it."

No, she's a broken person who breaks others to distract herself from how broken she is. Rebellion against all the things my mother represents has been one of my greatest acts of healing.

I'm more than aware of the drawbacks of going no-contact with my mother—trust me, I know the cultural taboo of estrangement; however, for the time being, it's the safest choice I can make. I have a right to choose who is and who is not in my life. People who judge me for protecting myself fall into the latter category.

During the summer of 2022, my dad gripped me like an octopus from the wiry bed of the urgent care. This marked the third or fourth time he'd gone through alcohol and opioid withdrawal in the last decade. Each time, there had been some injury that led to his being at the hospital, where booze and pills aren't taken freely, resulting in a weeks-to-months-long process of hell. But this time was different.

"Let me die! Let me die!" He writhed, kicking away the seven layers of hospital bedding to account for the sweats and shivers that come with delirium tremens.

"I know, I can see you're hurting, Daddy. I'm sorry," I cooed in a lower-register tone, hoping my voice might act like the Tibetan singing bowl I chimed each day to mark the beginning and end of my meditation. I made sure to use observation-forward statements to validate his pain, something I practiced while working with my students.

"Help me, D, help me," he pleaded. His hazel eyes bore a strange glaze, similar to the glaze over my late cat's eyes as the vet pushed down the needle of euthanization. How I wish I could help my dad. How I wish death didn't have to be so painful and ugly.

"I'm here, Daddy. I'm here."

But I was only there part-time. Inside, I was fantasizing about when I could escape back to my safety zone—solitude—so I could process this along with my guilt and shame at having stayed away for months at a time.

Since I moved back to Texas, going back home to Dallas has been an exercise in retraumatization. Every room of that house holds some memory—of rape, of drunken fights, of being shut down, of being hit, of being laughed at, of being shooed aside, of being pushed to grow up too damn fast. I've had panic attacks after every visit home.

I'm so used to pulling over to cry and shake on the side of I-35 that I just suck it up as a normal part of travel. I tried to change my tactic going into it via mental prep which I start about a week prior. How ridiculous to have to practice these things—to have to warm up like I'm running a marathon all to adhere to some role—daughter, sister, the "weird" one—I don't even want.

At the age of eighty-six, my father was formally diagnosed with Korsakoff's Syndrome, a nasty flavor of dementia caused by a lifetime of alcoholism. "Wet brain" is the fun term, as I discovered through Googling. The morbidly humorous image of a brain having a grand time in a swimming pool full of wine comes to mind. Then I think of that day after fourth-grade graduation, sitting beside the pool with my dad while he guffawed and poured Merlot into our pet rabbit's water bowl.

For a couple of weeks, he forgot he ever enjoyed alcohol. He forgot everything—he was a shell of himself. On one occasion, he even forgot my name. When we hugged, he was frail—not because he was thin, but because he was hollow.

~~~~~~

When people say, "You're so resilient!" I have to stop myself from replying, "Yeah, thanks for seeing my ability to endure a bunch of shit."

As a rich, white girl, my resilience feels cheap, like I haven't truly earned anything. I've been trained to minimize my experiences, robbing myself of the opportunity to mourn my traumas. It's considered naughty of me to have problems because look how pretty and wealthy, and therefore how easy, my life has been. In a society that puts wealth and beauty and the pursuit of happiness above everything, it seems all that society wants me to pursue is consumption and vanity...because I can. Is that resilience? Doing the expected?

The unexpected things often require the most expansion and, consequently, award the deepest lessons. Resilience is a word often used to judge one's ability to seem emotionally balanced when you're actually falling apart. I don't want this faux resilience. I want authenticity, vulnerability, and curiosity toward life's inherent suffering.

I'd be lying if I told you I was 100 percent healed. I still use substances—alcohol within reason, sometimes not within reason. I still have body dysmorphia. I catch myself checking my thighs or stomach—literally my uterus, which I believed was so fat for so long. I still have to navigate disordered thoughts at meals, the gym, or the grocery store. I still have severe anxiety over dentist appointments and health checkups. I still fear being found dead somewhere for myriad reasons out of my control.

The cool thing is that I've learned I can either act on those thoughts or say, "*Okay, okay, I see you, now on your way, buddy.*" Heavy emotions show the breadth of one's humanity. I'm proud I've learned to honor and carry them. And even though it's an icky thought, I feel slightly okay with the fact that they'll only get heavier with time. I'll become more human as a result.

With meditation, I realized I could drop into certain sections of my body and play witness to all the organized chaos occurring there. I visualized every tendon, every muscle fiber, loose or tight, whatever it may be. I visualized all the little tendrils that have woven together to create my body—what a marvel of nature it is!

After meditation, I make time to step outside. I see the little paths the ants braid, some carrying leaves and dirt clods larger than their bodies, others zipping by with a single grain of sand. Is there such a thing as suffering in the world of ants? Are the ones carrying plastic jealous of the ones carrying petals? What about the stragglers and the wanderers—have they rejected their assigned roles?

Chaos is found in every crevice of the natural world, common as feast and famine, dust and shadows, noise and silence.

~~~

In this account, I've purposely avoided numbers, details, and intense body imagery as to not trigger anyone else more than they already are triggered by their daily lives full of diets, food ads, the myth of perfection, and rampant body shaming. If anyone you know is struggling with body image or an eating disorder, don't comment on their body, don't try to be the food police, and don't attack or gossip about them. Nobody chooses to have an eating disorder. They are not a disorder, so don't treat them like one.

Instead, try to share with them a simple, sacred pause. The world is too noisy, too busy fixing and breaking. Playing silent witness to another person can work wonders. Listen and learn.

As much as I've shared about my parents' inadequacies, my beef isn't even with them because they, too, are victims of the hyper-capitalist Western society that creates conditions forcing strength and subsequent resilience upon us in the first place. I know deep down that my parents might just be lost, confused, emotionally disjointed, and trying their best with the tools they've been given. It's sad to see such shoddy craftsmanship, but, as I once heard a car mechanic proclaim, "I've learned a lot because I've fucked up a lot."

So don't tell me I'm resilient. Tell me I've fucked up enough. Enough to rest and to be still, to respond—not react—with grace to each flavor of suffering. Enough to now actively work on helping to build a society in which the majority can also say *I am enough.*

THE POWER OF *SANKOFA*

KRISTENE RUDDLE

"What time I am afraid, I will trust in thee." Psalms 56:3

This was the first Bible verse I memorized. As a child, I would awaken in the middle of the night feeling afraid. I would repeat this verse over and over until I was calm and able to go back to sleep. Bible verses, prayer, and a good sense of humor have stood the test of time in my life, helping me to endure many tough times and still find joy.

When I was growing up, I would often lay awake at night thinking about air raids. We lived in Fort Worth, Texas, near Carswell Air Force Base. I had a recurring dream about air raid sirens going off. The alarm would go off, and everyone in the house would jump up and run to the car. I would be the last one out, getting there just in time to see the car filled with my family driving away. Standing at the end of the driveway alone, I would watch the car leave me behind. Then a large dinosaur would appear and offer me a ride to the bomb shelter. This is when I would wake up. My heart would be pounding. I felt so alone and would repeat over and over, "What time I am afraid, I will trust in thee."

If I got a splinter in my finger, I would lie awake at night terrified that the splinter would enter my bloodstream and travel to my heart and kill me. Again, I would calm myself with this Bible verse and thankfully wake up in the morning alive.

During my childhood, I had to figure a lot of things out on my own. It saddens me to remember the emotional neglect my three siblings and I experienced. Our parents lived through the Depression and World War II and were a part of the "Greatest Generation." They did not talk about their lives and did not show much emotion.

When I was ten years old, my father woke up one morning, stood up, and then cried out in pain as he fell to the ground. He had lost the feeling in his right leg below his knee.

Because my father was a retired Lieutenant Colonel in the U.S. Army, my mother took him to the hospital at Carswell Air Force Base. The test results showed a blocked artery in the right leg below his knee. The vein had collapsed, and gangrene had set in. My father was transferred to Lackland Air Force Base in San Antonio, Texas, for surgery to amputate his leg.

My mother stayed with my father during the week and came home to check on us once or twice a month on weekends. Our grandmother or aunt stayed with us the remainder of the time. Six months later, our aunt called us children into the living room.

"Your father needs surgery, and it is not certain if he will live. Whatever you do, don't cry, and don't talk to your mother about it."

I teared up and struggled to not let anyone see my tears. Only a few hours later, we got the news that my father had died.

177

A few weeks after my father's funeral, I felt the need to cry. I found a place behind a privacy fence next to our house. I sat on the ground curled up in a fetal position and cried a prayer, "Thank you, God, for being with me. Please help me. I'm so sad right now."

Suddenly, it felt like I was being held in God's loving arms. Even today, I can feel the sorrow of that child and feel God's arms wrapped around her, comforting her.

~~~~~

After my father's death, for the next seven years I lived in a fog of depression. I tried to get out of my depressed state by pursuing a future in nursing. I became a candy striper in high school, and after I graduated, I took classes in the nursing program at Texas Christian University. But what was I thinking? I was miserable when I realized that I fainted at the sight of blood, threw up at bad smells, and had little empathy for sick people.

Now discouraged even more, I quit school and found a job as a secretary. It was while I was doing secretarial work that I met my husband, Lynn, at First Baptist Church of Benbrook, a suburb of Fort Worth, Texas. I was attracted to him as he charismatically served as a lay evangelist, either preaching or leading the singing. Lynn quickly became my best friend. We married in 1968 when I was nineteen years old. At my young age, I naively assumed that being married meant experiencing love, having children, and spending a long life together. In the early months of our marriage, we had fun together and often hosted friends for potluck dinners or game nights. Our friends told us that we seemed to have a perfect marriage; I sure agreed with them.

Six months after we married, we loaded all our possessions into our new purple Duster and moved to Pendleton, Oregon, to help build a Southern Baptist church. I loved Oregon and have many good memories of our five years there, including the births of our two sons Brent and Scott.

My first pregnancy was extremely difficult—in fact, both my son Brent and I almost died due to my loss of blood. Throughout the long ordeal, Lynn did not show much emotion, but he later showed me a check that he started to write while at a hospital restaurant. Instead of writing the name of the restaurant, he had written, "It's a boy!" He was clearly proud to be a dad. We had been a couple, but now we were a family.

My second pregnancy, two years later, was much easier. On March 30, 1973, Scott was born by C-section. While Lynn and I welcomed him into our family, Brent was not sure about this new addition as he thought Scott should be able to play with him right away. I often would find him sitting in the crib with a baseball glove or ball watching his baby brother.

After five years in Oregon, we moved back to Fort Worth. We lived near family, joined another Southern Baptist church, participated in church activities, and made many friends. During this time, I enjoyed being a stay-at-home mother. I attended a women's Bible study group at our church. During my prayer time, I often felt led to pray for my husband. I was confused by this because he seemed to be doing well. He was a leader at our church. He had a good job. He was well liked.

But my burden to pray for him did not go away, so I made a commitment to fast and pray for him one day each week.

One day during my prayer time, I received a remarkable vision that revealed that in the future I would minister to women in some way. I had no idea what that meant, but this vision remained with me.

The next time I met with my women's Bible study group, Marilyn, the leader, looked around the room. Then she said, "God has impressed upon me that someone in this group has been called to a ministry for women. Who has felt this calling recently?"

I couldn't believe her words! With my heart pounding, I hesitantly raised my hand. "I have. In my prayer time, I felt God speak to me and say I would someday have a ministry to women."

Marilyn nodded affirmatively. "We will pray for you, Kristene." The women gathered around me and prayed for me asking God's blessings and protection on my life.

After working in Texas for five years, my husband decided he wanted to change careers and take a job in sales. In 1978, he obtained a new job as a regional sales manager for a tool company, a job that moved us to Greenwood, Indiana. Being from Texas, we were so excited about the prospect of finally seeing a lot of snow. But I sure didn't know that I was going to face a different type of blizzard.

The first few years in Indiana went by in a whirl. The boys were in elementary school with Brent in third grade and Scott in kindergarten. Scott was mad that he only attended half-day kindergarten since he wanted to do everything his older brother did. Lynn was a success at his new job and was often recognized for being the best salesman. He was a leader in our church, sang in the choir, and led a Sunday School class. I taught a women's Bible study class.

All seemed good. Yet, I still felt the burden to pray for Lynn each day, and I continued to fast one day every week.

In 1980, I noticed some changes in my husband's personality. He would be fine one moment, then forgetful and sometimes moody. His anger was usually directed towards himself. Mostly he withdrew and didn't respond to questions about how he felt or what was going on.

One Saturday, in search of some books that might help me understand his personality changes, I drove to the Greenwood Public Library. That morning as I sat in my car in front of the library, I sensed in my spirit a premonition that something bad was going to happen. I remember praying and telling God that whatever it was, I would trust in Him. I felt God say to me, "If you will follow me, you and your children will be okay."

When I got home from the library, my husband asked to speak to me. As we sat at the kitchen table, Lynn looked at me and said, "I have a problem with alcohol."

"What do you mean?" I asked.

He sighed. "It started after I went to the dentist and experienced a high from laughing gas. The next time I went out of town on business, I bought a large bottle of wine. I drank the entire bottle quickly and experienced the same enjoyable high as I did from the laughing gas." He said he continued to buy alcohol every time he traveled. Since he traveled every week, he was drinking heavily every week.

"Please forgive me," he said with tears in his eyes. "Please pray for me."

We held hands and prayed together. Afterwards, I thought everything was going to be okay.

~~~

As the months and eventually years passed, it became evident that asking for forgiveness, praying, and supporting one another did not end Lynn's addiction to alcohol. At the time, I did not know anything about substance abuse, so I decided to learn everything that I could about alcoholism.

I found the book *Another Chance: Hope and Health for the Alcoholic Family,* by Sharon Wegscheider-Cruse, to be an important eye opener to the disease. It describes how alcoholism impacts children and shares the roles that children play in an alcoholic family. I recognized these roles as ones that my siblings and I had played in my family as we grew up, even though to my knowledge neither my mother nor father were alcoholics. However, both my parents had an extensive history of alcoholism in their families, and Lynn's family also had a history of substance abuse and mental illness. As I thought about our family histories, it began to make sense that I had married someone with an addiction.

Lynn was a "closet alcoholic." He only drank in secret when he was out of town or when he could hide the bottles in our house. When I confronted him with any bottles that I found, he would deny that they were his. He also began a pattern of changing jobs often, working just long enough for the health insurance to kick in. Then he would go on a drinking binge and end up in the hospital with alcohol poisoning.

In the early years of his alcoholism, we went through a substance abuse treatment program at Central State Hospital in Indianapolis. It was in this treatment program that I learned about resources for families of alcoholics and attended my first Al-Anon meeting.

I was angry with God when I attended my first Al-Anon meeting *What had I done to deserve this? Why were my children being exposed to their father's behavior?* The Al-Anon members encouraged me to attend six meetings before deciding if the group was something I should stick with. After attending six meetings, I was still angry. I also hated that they referred to God as a "Higher Power" and not as God. At the end of that sixth meeting, we stood in a circle and a young woman said, "If you quit, we will gladly refund your misery."

It only took a few more months of living with active alcoholism for me to be at my wits end. I was miserable enough to return to the Al-Anon meetings, and this time I kept attending. I no longer cared how they referred to God. I no longer cared if Lynn's alcoholism was my fault or not my fault. I knew I needed help. The members of Al-Anon took me in just as I was. I read the Al-Anon devotional *One Day at a Time* every day. As I gained insight into myself and the effects of alcoholism, I began to heal. Most importantly, I learned that I was not alone.

In 1981, my husband started to attend AA meetings and found a sponsor. He just never quit drinking. Eventually after being in several treatment programs, he was hospitalized for psychiatric problems and diagnosed with a bipolar disorder. After several more psychiatric hospitalizations, he was also diagnosed with a personality disorder.

It became evident that he was not going to stop drinking nor was he going to work and provide for his family.

This left me with a difficult decision to make. I knew someone needed to work to provide income. And I knew it had to be me. I had been a stay-at-home mom for twelve years and did not have a college education. I was unsure if I could find a job. But I had worked as a unit secretary at Harris Hospital in Fort Worth, Texas, after high school graduation. That experience now garnered me a position as a secretary at Valle Vista Hospital, a new psychiatric hospital in Greenwood, Indiana. I felt that God had opened the right door for me.

What should I do next? I wanted to live a "normal" life. We were living in a house that was in foreclosure because we had not paid a mortgage payment for over eighteen months. I don't know why we were able to live in the house that long, but I knew it wasn't right. I made the decision to move out with the boys and found us a small rental home. Out of sympathy for him, I told Lynn he could come live with us—although I hoped he wouldn't. He wasn't working, and most of the time he was drunk, passed out, or sitting and staring into space. He decided to join us.

It was at this time that I came to a very dark place in my faith journey and relationship with God. I recall in a prayer time telling God how I felt: "I have done everything I could to be your obedient child. I feel the rules laid out in Scripture have failed me. My church family does not know how to offer support to me or to my children."

One day while feeling quite hopeless and afraid of what ball might drop next, I suddenly remembered the verse I had memorized from my childhood: "What time I am afraid, I will trust in thee." I needed to still trust in God. Right then, I made a conscious decision to continue to believe in God's goodness, faithfulness, and protection, no matter how difficult my circumstances were.

Then the final straw came that helped me decide to end my marriage. The explosion of the space shuttle Challenger on January 28, 1986, sent my husband into a deep depression. Lynn sat in a room with the curtains drawn and the lights turned off for several days. I finally sat down with him.

"You need to tell me what's wrong."

"You know about the disaster of the Challenger exploding? It was my fault."

I sure was not expecting this fantastical explanation! "What do you mean, it was your fault?"

"I have been a spy since I was in college. It was my job to deliver a message about the O rings to NASA. I failed."

This was too much to take. Even though I know his delusions came from his illness, I went to see a lawyer to help me understand my options if I decided to get a divorce.

In a straightforward voice, the attorney said, "You need to make a choice. You can take care of your husband, or you can take care of your sons."

That made the decision a little easier. As much as I still loved my husband, there was no choice between him and our children. The children needed a parent, and he was not going to be that parent. By this time, the boys were teenagers. I suspected that they blamed me for the problems created by their father's drinking. They also looked to me to make everything okay, and this was one time I could try to do that.

My hope and prayer for my sons was that they would know they were loved and that I believed in them.

Initially, I asked my husband to leave. He did not leave willingly, but eventually he left, ending up in a psychiatric hospital after another overdose of alcohol. From there, he went to live in a halfway house. During this time, I filed for separation. When his behavior and attitude did not change, I filed for divorce. He made it clear that he wanted a divorce but was not going to pay for it. The divorce was finalized in September of 1987.

~~~

I was now a single mother raising two teenage sons by myself. According to the terms of our divorce agreement, their father could see them whenever he wanted to. Within six months of our divorce, their father remarried, and we learned his new wife was pregnant. Brent went to stay with them on two occasions but asked to come home early due to the discomfort in their home. My youngest son Scott decided he wanted nothing to do with his father.

Brent started drinking when he was close to sixteen. He had several incidents related to his drinking in his teens and was suspended from school a few times. We participated in counseling together; I don't know if it helped him, but at the least I think it kept the door open to his establishing a better relationship with me.

One week before Brent's high school graduation, his English teacher called me. "Mrs. Ruddle, I'm very sorry, but Brent does not have enough points to pass this class." She asked me whether she should pass him or not, as he was close to receiving a passing grade.

My heart broke, but I knew what I needed to tell her. "No, please don't pass him. Brent needs to take responsibility for not doing his work." So Brent did not graduate with his high school class; instead, he enrolled in summer school so that he could earn his diploma. He also decided to meet with a recruiter and sign up to join the Marines after he graduated.

The last week of summer school Brent was suspended by the vice principal who saw him holding an unlit cigarette in the school parking lot. The suspension made it impossible for Brent to graduate. When this happened, he reached out to the Marine recruiter who picked him up from school. The recruiter called me, told me what had happened, and asked, "Mrs. Ruddle, would you allow Brent to remain at home this fall semester to take the classes he needs to graduate?"

I knew this was another time to show tough love. "No, I can't do it. He'll need to go live with his father, who now lives in Texas with his parents." By this time, I knew that I had exhausted all efforts on my part to help Brent. I felt if I continued to let him live at home, I was enabling him to continue to make the poor choices that he had been making. Even though I knew living with his father was not a good option, I didn't know what else to do.

Thankfully, the recruiter also knew that living with his father was not an acceptable option, so he allowed Brent to join the Marines without his high school diploma.

Brent was very angry when he left home for the Marines. He let me know this through getting drunk, cussing me out, and damaging my car. I understood where his hurt and anger came from. He had a good relationship with his father before Lynn's drinking escalated, and I know it was hard for Brent to understand the changes in his dad. The hard part for me was knowing I could not change things for him or heal his wounds. I continued to pray for Brent and Scott and never gave up hope. Looking at their baby pictures and remembering them as happy children playing together helped me keep my hope alive.

When Brent got out of basic training, he called to apologize for his behavior towards me. I could hear the excitement in his voice as he shared his challenges and accomplishments. "Mom, you aren't so bad. And you were right, I did kick the dent in the door of your car." He ended the call with, "I love you."

During his service in the Marines, Brent served in the Gulf War on board a Navy carrier. It was a stressful time for both of us as it was for our nation. When the war was over, he returned to Camp Pendleton in San Diego where he completed his service. Before his discharge, he was offered the opportunity to complete a substance abuse recovery program. After completing the program, he was honorably discharged.

When Brent returned home from the Marines, he lived with me for a while. He immediately enrolled in night school, completed the required classes, and earned his high school diploma. He even proudly made a trip to his high school to show the school counselor his diploma.

But sadly, Brent continued to drink, and it soon became apparent that I was enabling him by allowing him to live with me. So, I told Brent he had to move out. At the time, he was engaged to get married. He and his fiancé moved in together and had their first child, a daughter. Then they married and had their second child, a son. I was so happy to finally have grandchildren.

Eventually Brent's marriage ended, and because his ex-wife worked nights, the children stayed with Brent during the week. Brent was a good father when he wasn't drinking, but as his drinking escalated, I worried about his children. I debated several times whether I should call Child Protective Services. As I struggled with this decision, Brent was involved in a DUI and was arrested in the middle of the night. The police called me, and I went to pick up the children. I called their mother to let her know that they were with me, and she could pick them up when she got off work.

Brent took this situation in stride; it was not a wake-up call for him, and he did not quit drinking. He was able to work, usually as a bartender in a restaurant. He started dating again and eventually married a young woman he met at one of the restaurants. She already had two young children, so on weekends he watched his two children and his two stepchildren. Unfortunately, his new wife participated in drinking and smoking marijuana with him. After some time, this marriage also eventually ended in divorce.

During the time that Brent was spiraling out of control, his younger brother Scott thankfully was doing well. Scott graduated from high school and attended Purdue University on a scholarship. His high school girlfriend went to a different college for one year but then transferred to attend Purdue.

I was inspired by Scott's college life. When he left home to attend college in 1991, I decided to take a class at a nearby university to see if I could handle the work. I found that I loved being back in school, so

I continued to take more classes. For the next six years, I worked full time at a psychiatric hospital and took two classes each semester until I graduated with a bachelor's degree in social work. Ultimately, this led to my completing a master's degree in Applied Sociology and earning a living doing what I had always done for free—helping people with their problems.

Scott and his girlfriend both graduated from Purdue in 1996, got married, and then began their life together. Scott found a job at a bank, and his wife taught kindergarten. Scott changed jobs several times, but he remained in the field of finance. Their marriage seemed to be strong. After a couple of years, they bought their first home and had their first child. They eventually had two boys and a girl and decided that they would adopt a baby girl from China. I was grateful that I had one son who did not abuse drugs. Scott's family was very involved in the church that his wife had grown up in, and he was elected an elder and youth leader.

One day, I heard that Scott was smoking marijuana. When I talked to him about this, he did not see it as a problem, although he was keeping his behavior a secret from his wife. I was heartbroken and knew that I couldn't hide my feelings about it. I asked him to tell her—and gave him a deadline—or I would tell her. He waited till the last minute, but he told her. He also told her how he felt he could use marijuana to earn more money for their family.

As the years passed, I increasingly realized that my living so close to my sons was not helping them. I also learned that my older sister, Cookie, was fighting breast cancer. Since she lived alone, she needed some support. In 2011, she invited me to move to Dallas and live with her as she knew that I needed a fresh start. I had always said that I would never live in Texas; it was way too hot, and the people in Dallas drove like maniacs. I sure have learned to be careful about saying "never!"

I lived with my sister for three years and then moved into an apartment of my own. I enjoyed attending church services at Royal Lane Baptist Church; the love and acceptance of the church family was refreshing and a healing balm to my soul. I found a wonderful women's Sunday School class to attend, and I eventually led the class. For years, the women in the class prayed with me for my sons. Their prayers were a great support.

When I left Indiana, things worsened for both Scott and Brent. Scott had a business partner in several business ventures, one of which involved selling marijuana. Scott's focus was now on making money and using drugs, and he involved his brother Brent in some of his schemes. They drove to California to buy marijuana plants and then drove them back to Indiana.

On one of the trips, Brent and a friend were stopped by a sheriff in Texas. The sheriff found the marijuana plants, a handgun, and $40,000 in his car. Brent and his friend spent the weekend in jail until his brother bailed him out.

Because he had nowhere else to live, Lynn was now living with Brent in my home. But not for long. One night he overdosed and died of alcohol poisoning. Brent found his father's body in the bedroom, but he was in no condition to do anything about it. Thankfully, Scott stepped in and called 911.

Once Lynn's body was released, the boys had him cremated. Then they made a trip to Texas and held a small gathering of family and friends at Benbrook Lake to share memories of Lynn and to release his ashes at the lake's shore. For me, this was bittersweet. I was grateful that they did this for their father, yet it emphasized the loss of the good man Lynn was before his drinking began.

After his father's death, whenever I spoke with Brent by phone, it was evident that his drinking was increasing. He was unable to make the house payments—nor could I. I had no choice but to sell the house, and Brent eventually ended up homeless.

Scott quickly asked, "Mom, what can I do for him? How can I help him?"

I encouraged Scott to take Brent to a homeless program in downtown Indianapolis that specialized in helping veterans. Thankfully, Brent agreed to go with his brother to Horizon House, a day center for the homeless. With the help of a case manager, Brent was referred to a program for veterans.

A few weeks later, Brent called to tell me that he had moved into his own place, and it was great. He said that one of the requirements to keep it was that he had to attend Alcoholics Anonymous meetings.

"I'll go, but I'm not going to stop drinking," he told me.

One Sunday night, he called after attending an AA meeting. I had never heard him so excited and full of joy. He had finally found a home and supportive friends.

When Brent first started attending AA meetings, his sponsor and AA friends told him that to achieve sobriety, he needed to cut off contact with his brother. It was very difficult for him to do this as he and Scott had always been close. At first, he did not understand why this was necessary, but he eventually saw the wisdom in it and was able to set healthy boundaries with Scott.

Brent was hired for a good job, but when they did a background check, they had to let him go. Then he learned there was a warrant out for his arrest in both Indiana and Texas, so he turned himself in. Texas sent officers to Indianapolis to escort Brent back to face the charges from the drug bust in 2011.

In 2014, Brent began serving a two-year sentence for his drug charges. As we were both now living in Texas, I visited Brent often in prison. It was meaningful to have this time with him. I trusted God with his safety and journey and was proud of the way he handled his prison sentence with courage and wisdom. His AA sponsor in Indiana also came to visit him every year for his sobriety anniversary which meant a great deal to him.

He participated in several programs offered by the prison, and when he was released on parole, he left with both a support group and a job. Thankfully, Brent has been sober every day since then, one day at a time.

Unfortunately, back in Indiana Scott's drug use was worsening. It was evident that Scott was now neglecting his family in the same way that his father had neglected us. I was angry that both of my sons had abused drugs and been greatly influenced by their father's addiction despite all my efforts to help them. I did not want my anger to destroy our relationships. I knew I needed help.

In my work as an advocate at a domestic violence agency, I had the privilege of attending training on substance abuse. I knew I needed a counselor who understood addiction and who practiced EMDR, Eye

Movement Desensitization and Reprocessing Therapy. Thankfully, I found someone competent to work with me. We traveled back to my earliest childhood memories as well as to my current relationships with my sons and their families. Each session highlighted my life-time of always feeling responsible for everyone's well-being. I realized that some of my anger was directed at myself. Through this therapy I learned three important lessons: I needed to let go of my expectations, I needed to grieve my losses, and most importantly, I needed to take better care of myself.

After spending a week with Scott and his family at their home in Indiana, I shared my concerns with my counselor about my son's abusive treatment of his wife and children. A short time later, Scott was arrested for selling drugs and was sentenced to prison. When this happened, his wife made the tough decision to separate from him. After a year, Scott was released and put into a treatment center. Thankfully, he continued in the outreach program and stayed in contact with his sponsor.

Scott never returned home, and he and his wife are now divorced. He has standard visitation with his youngest child, the only child who never excluded him from her life. His older children stayed away from him at different times, but now that he is sober, they all spend some time with him regularly.

Today, Brent is back home in Indiana, has a good job, continues attending AA meetings, and has regular visits with his children. Recently, his daughter asked him to walk her down the aisle at her wedding. She wrote him a letter telling him how at one time she did not think she would even be able to ask him to attend her wedding, but he changed his life, and she was so proud of him.

As I write this, I feel deep gratitude for both of my sons' sobriety

~⸻~

and growth. Knowing that their father did not have any involvement in their lives after our divorce, I am especially proud of them for making efforts to stay involved in their children's lives. They both recognize the need for repairing relationships, and thankfully, they are learning to relate to their adult children.

I have learned to cherish the time we share and to realize that my sons are not their addictions. Underneath the disease of their substance abuse, they are men of great value. Since their births, I've learned so much from them and know that not one lesson I've learned has been wasted.

I often think back to my earlier life when I felt called to minister to women. It's been a blessing to see how that calling has been actualized throughout my life.

Today, I use these lessons as I work as an advocate at the Genesis Women's Shelter, a non-profit that serves women and children who have been impacted by partner violence. For the past eleven years, it has been my privilege to advocate for women who have the courage to ask for help. Yes, it is challenging work, especially in my mid-seventies, but it is a joy to be helpful to others. It's been gratifying to see that so many of the hardships I faced as a wife and a mother have given me tools to help women in similar situations.

When I was in college, I was introduced to an African symbol that deeply resonated with me—a mythical bird with its feet firmly planted forward and its head turned backwards. It is the principle of *Sankofa*, which is derived from the people of Ghana.

It represents the idea that *one should remember the past to make positive progress in the future.* The power of *Sankofa* centers around this idea: To know your history and your heritage is to know your current self, the world around you, and how to better both.

This is the principle I still try to live by. I pray that I'll continue to learn from my history, so I'll know myself more fully. And through this knowledge, I hope to continue to better the lives of those around me.

THE LONG RIDE HOME

LINDA DEAN MCDERMITT

The child must know that he is a miracle, that since the beginning of the world there hasn't been, and until the end of the world there will not be, another child like him.

—Pablo Casals

Leaving the hospital without my baby, I knew my life as it was and as it might have been had changed. I had experienced pain and known loneliness, but the depth of *this* was unbearable. How could I leave her there, hovering precariously between this world and the next with a ventilator breathing for her, with multiple IVs delivering medications, and not knowing the pain she might be experiencing?

If you knew my story, you might think the moment that changed my life was when in the middle of my pregnancy Dr. J. told my husband Michael and me that something was terribly wrong with our baby. The doctors diagnosed Sarah with a diaphragmatic hernia (d-hernia), a rare congenital condition that is often linked to a chromosomal disorder. But what did that mean?

After that day in August, I knew Sarah was in danger, but I was in denial. Even following a meeting with Dr. R., a pioneering pediatric surgeon, I failed to comprehend what pulmonary hypotension and the use of ECMO (extracorporeal membrane oxygenation—heart-lung by-pass) would mean. My mind refused to let my thoughts delve deeply enough to know how sick Sarah could be as she entered this life. We planned and prepared, attended baby showers, and decorated her nursery. I played a game of pretend, but there were moments that I saved for her darkened nursery where I cried tears of despair and pleaded with whatever entity might know my anguish to keep Sarah healthy and whole.

The day before Sarah's birth, I was leaking fluid, so the on-call perinatologist instructed me to go to the hospital. Once at Presbyterian Hospital Labor and Delivery, a technician performed an ultrasound, and the doctor informed me that my uterus was seeping amniotic fluid. Sarah's ability to swallow amniotic fluid and then urinate it back into the amniotic sac was impaired because her stomach and intestines had pushed through the hole in her diaphragm and into her chest; my fluid levels had increased beyond normal capacity, stretching my uterus to its limits.

At only thirty-five weeks, the plan included bedrest and keeping Sarah in utero as long as possible to enhance her development and size, especially of her lungs. Sarah had other plans. My water broke that night, and contractions began. Prior to the pushing stage, the neonatologist came into the room to give me Sarah's prognosis: she had a fifty-fifty chance of survival.

As I began pushing, the room crowded with doctors and medical technicians. As soon as Sarah was born, she needed immediate medical attention. I heard no cries. They intubated her and started IVs and a central line.

Over the next five days, liquid oxygen filled her lungs, and she underwent surgery while on ECMO to provide a Gore-Tex barrier between her chest cavity and her digestive organs. Shifting her stomach and intestines from the chest would provide space for her left lung to grow and develop; at the time, it was less than a third of normal size.

As we drove home from the hospital following Sarah's birth, I felt emptiness and shock. We stopped briefly to pick up a breast pump so that I could provide milk for Sarah in the near future. It felt like that was one of the only things I could do that might benefit her. We weren't on any normal timeline. This was no sprint. This was going to be an endurance race, a lifetime journey. And when we walked through the door of our dark, quiet house, I knew life as I had known it had changed forever.

~ ~

I had grown up as the youngest in a Southern Baptist family of five and as the daughter of parents who had lived through the Depression and World War II. I was a change-of-life baby coming to parents already in their mid-forties. I shared a deep closeness with my father while I often felt like a nuisance to my mother. Normal childhood behaviors such as asking questions, reading books, and playing sports were activities she saw as rebellious and unladylike. When the questions turned to religion, the books to more questions, and the sports to boys, even my relationship with my daddy strained under the weight of my growing independence. And yet I lived at home with them until my twenty-seventh year—through college, my first jobs, early romantic and not-so-romantic liaisons, and the realization that I was not going to be a daughter who followed my parents' path to salvation and traditional values. I had little interest in marrying or having children.

During my single years, my questions about religion and the spiritual realm deepened and expanded. I wanted to believe something. Regardless of the truths I thought I was uncovering, I couldn't let go of the religion of my upbringing—or it wouldn't let go of me. The longing I felt had more to do with a time of childlike acceptance, of listening to hymns, of feeling emotions that entangled guilt and fear with love and gave rise to an underlying anger that kept joy at bay. The answers I was given at church simply didn't add up the way I needed them to.

Following a string of relationships and time spent drifting and drinking, I stopped seeking the flirtations and incompatibilities of serious and casual liaisons. I stopped frequenting bars and nightclubs. Almost immediately, I met someone. *The* someone. I already knew Michael as a supervisor in another division of the Internal Revenue Service where I worked. We met after work one day and went to dinner the next night. The way he looked at me made my heart leap. There was so much love and acceptance in his beautiful blue-green eyes. His deep, gentle voice at the end of the phone line thrilled me. This was it.

We dated a year before being married by a justice of the peace and moving from Dallas to Austin. This move created further distance between my family and me. I missed them and my friends, but Michael and I loved spending time together sharing movies, music, and football. Life was relatively easy with little conflict.

After about three-and-a-half years, we moved back to Dallas, and within the year, we were expecting Sarah. I thought I would take time off from work to stay home with two children until they reached school age. We'd take vacations and spend time with our family as we worked on strengthening our relationships.

Although I wouldn't say my career working for the IRS was a driving force in my life, I enjoyed my work as a human resources assistant and anticipated eventually going back to work, whether at the IRS, another government agency, or somewhere in the private sector.

When anyone starts a family, changes in their self-identity occur. For me, the shift of learning to think of someone else's well-being before my own came nineteen weeks into my pregnancy. My well-being became inseparably entwined with Sarah's. The diagnosis of her d-hernia meant frequent visits with a perinatologist. I also experienced gestational diabetes which meant following a closely monitored diet and blood sugar checks. I became fully consumed with taking care of myself in order to care for Sarah.

Deciding to follow through with a pregnancy was a tremendous commitment and responsibility, which is why having that choice was integral to shaping how I moved forward.

My obstetrician ensured us that the choice to terminate my pregnancy was available to me and Michael and was solely ours to make. I was in a loving relationship, and we were equipped with financial and educational resources to care for Sarah. And because there was some hope for our daughter, we decided to continue my pregnancy. Not everyone would have made the same decision, and I completely support other couples' right to decide differently.

Sarah was born on Sunday, December 8, 1996. Doctors immediately intubated her and took her to the Level IV Neonatal Intensive Care Unit, the unit that accommodated the most critically ill neonates. We entered a surreal world of medical guessing and miracles, along with emotional mood swings.

Although we couldn't have known it at the time, nearly a year-long hospital stay for Sarah lay ahead of us. During that span, she would undergo five life-threatening surgeries.

On the morning of January 4, nearly a full month after her birth, Michael and I were finally each allowed a brief time to hold Sarah. We wondered if it would be our only chance to feel her precious life in our hands. We had seen other families in the NICU grieving the loss of their babies. It all seemed too horrible to be real. How could this be the will of God or of any all-loving, all-powerful, all-knowing God? In solitude, I wept and sought forgiveness for anything I could have done that placed this burden on Sarah. With the vision of her swollen, bruised, and helpless body in my mind, I pleaded with the Universe for her healing.

Days later, fluid built up in the pericardial sac surrounding her heart, and her heart couldn't pump efficiently, straining other organ activity. Dr. W., Sarah's pediatric cardiologist, explained that Sarah needed open-heart surgery to drain the fluid, an operation that only a different hospital could provide. Not only was the surgery life-threatening, but also the transport between the two hospitals was as well.

One of the neonatologists held my arm and comforted me. "No one has ever done anything so bad to have their baby go through this," he told me. *How did he know where my thoughts had taken me?*

Sarah survived the surgery but was still in critical condition. Dr. W. came out to talk to us. "Every baby deserves a chance. Until her heart is working properly, nothing else will."

In the middle of January, edema increased again, and other numbers started moving in the wrong direction. Sarah reached the point where she weighed thirteen pounds, but five of those pounds was fluid. Her eyes were swollen shut.

Dr. G., Sarah's primary neonatologist, cautioned, "We're doing all we can think of to do for Sarah." She was telling us to prepare ourselves. In under two months of life, Sarah had been at death's door on almost a daily basis.

Sarah's body finally started responding to treatment. She experienced brief periods of alertness. But her body couldn't shake off the need for positive air pressure. By the end of March, she was sporting a tracheostomy tube to help her breathe and allow for more positive oral manipulation to enhance the possibility of eating and talking.

Dr. G. tried to get a handle on our insurance coverage for at-home care. If Sarah went home now, she would need a ventilator and appropriate medical personnel to assist us in caring for her. Not only would the insurance company not cover in-home nursing care, but it also had a lifetime cap on durable medical equipment which would be used up within the first few years of Sarah's life. We knew how fortunate we were to have such good health insurance; many people have no health insurance at all. For the near future, Sarah remained hospitalized.

Nurses taught me how to care for our medically fragile child. I learned to suction secretions from her trache tube and do trache care, including removing and replacing it. Spending time in the NICU brought me into contact with some of the most compassionate and gifted medical personnel I have ever known.

Before I fell asleep at night, I often questioned how this could have happened. I wondered why Sarah had to go through so much pain and difficulty. *Could I be and do all that she needed?* And I was angry, too! Throughout our most trying times, people often tried to comfort us by speaking about some profound reason behind all of this. Some told us that God knew what He was doing when He gave Sarah to us. My inner quarrel over how this plan could be divine still rages in my thoughts today.

We started attending services at a Unity church and often experienced a much-needed sense of peace there, though strong emotions also rose to the surface. Its philosophy and openness differed quite a bit from the conservative Baptist upbringing of my youth.

I gradually took on a role as "NICU den mother." Dr. Elizabeth asked me to attend parent meetings, not only for myself but also for what I might offer other parents starting down a similar path with their newborn. Exposing my own fragility and fears gave me strength. It's the kind of strength I never sought to prove, but it sustained me.

Up until July, Sarah had either received her nutrition through an IV or a nasogastric (NG) tube. Doctors recommended a Nissen surgery to tighten the sphincter between the esophagus and the stomach and a procedure to create an opening in her stomach for a feeding tube. A few days prior to her surgery, Sarah's NG tube became displaced.

She choked and stopped breathing. It was nearly twenty minutes before she could be revived.

The surgery continued as planned, and we spent the next few months focused on stabilizing and improving Sarah's condition: tweaking respiratory settings for supplemental oxygen and pressures, helping her gain weight, and proceeding with occupational and physical therapies.

Most new mothers have an opportunity for skin-to-skin contact immediately following birth. Sarah and I both missed out on this beneficial physiological and psychological stage of connection. Nurse D. watched me holding Sarah while she slept on top of me in one of the NICU recliners and asked if I'd like to do skin-to-skin with Sarah. I removed my blouse, and she lay Sarah back on my chest.

At that moment, after all we'd been through, I felt most like her mother than at any other time.

Going to the hospital daily took a heavy toll on us. Michael and I were both physically and psychologically exhausted. Michael compartmentalized Sarah's adversities from his work; it gave him a respite of sorts. Occasionally, he had to travel for work. When a business trip came up in San Francisco, the nurses encouraged us to both go. That was November 1997. It would be our last vacation together.

On Monday of Thanksgiving week, when Sarah was just over eleven months old, the NICU team threw us a going-home party. We thanked everyone for their expertise, dedication, and love. They were Sarah's family, and when we couldn't be there, they were her angels on earth.

Dr. H., her pediatric nephrologist, told us, "It was all Sarah; she wanted so much to be here."

Michael asked Nurse C., Sarah's primary nurse, "What chance did you give Sarah on a scale of one to ten following her transport to Medical City Hospital from Presbyterian Hospital for heart surgery?"

"Zero," she frankly answered.

Dr. Elizabeth told the group, "In all my years as a family therapist, I have never seen a baby as sick as Sarah survive and go home."

Dr. S. humbly added, "She brought us to our knees."

The Tuesday before Thanksgiving, after almost an entire year in the hospital, we brought our baby girl home. I had no idea how hard life was about to become.

～∾～

My identity was now absorbed into Sarah's. I wanted so much to be a mother, but I never planned on being a nurse/therapist/teacher with little to no sleep and a shrinking outside life. Sarah's rigorous schedule of tube feedings, breathing treatments, medication administrations, tracheostomy care, physical, occupational, and speech therapy, and medical appointments kept me awake from before 6:00 a.m. to after 12:00 midnight. Between those times her pulse oximeter alarm often sounded, pulling me from precious sleep as I readjusted her position or assessed whatever else she might need.

Depression soon kicked in, but I couldn't see it. I had drunk quite a bit of alcohol in my college years, but I knew I couldn't afford to turn to it now with Sarah depending on me for so much.

Sadly, I unintentionally turned away from Michael as I devoted myself completely to Sarah's care. I slept in Sarah's bedroom with her for many months; then I moved into the bedroom next to her for an extended time.

Slowly, Michael and I started to drift apart. I didn't feel like a wife anymore and didn't know how to act like one. Even as we became Team Sarah, Michael and I both grieved our diminished personal relationship.

I didn't feel I could ask for help from anyone. In the months that Sarah had been hospitalized, I could count on two hands the number of times my family that lived close to us in the Dallas area had visited us. When I was growing up, asking for help was frowned upon in our family. I knew a few of my friends wanted to help, but they didn't know how.

Time at home passed with extreme highs and lows. Only now there were more highs than lows. Sarah underwent another major surgery at eighteen-months of age. This bold procedure allowed her to gradually wean off supplemental oxygen and her CPAP (Continuous Positive Airway Pressure) machine. This set the stage for more stamina, better mobility, and developmental progress.

My mother's health failed in 1998, and less than a year after Sarah came home from the hospital, Momma passed away. Her death emphasized our isolation; at her funeral we saw many family members and friends we hadn't seen in ages, and I realized how much I was missing that contact.

When Sarah turned three, we learned from her 1999 MRI that a portion of her brain tissue had been injured or had died. Her developmental outlook was disheartening. The developmental specialist speculated that Sarah would probably never walk or talk. Again, I sank into a pit of hopelessness. I tried to tell myself that Sarah was unlike any other baby. She moved to her own rhythm, and maybe she really would be okay.

When we lived in Texas' Collin County, we had free in-home therapeutic resources at our disposal. Several women came to our home regularly to work with Sarah—occupational, physical, and speech therapists, along with a visual impairment (VI) instructor. These women were simply amazing! Not only did Sarah make developmental improvements—sitting up, crawling, grasping, attending, standing—but visiting with them brightened my day.

In the spring of 2000, Sarah's speech therapist asked me to speak to a class of burgeoning therapists at the University of Texas at Dallas and give them a parent's perspective on how a special needs child can affect the family, helping them understand what parents experience during grueling long-term hospital care and the unplanned in-home impacts. My throat tightened with emotion as I spoke, and they were visibly shaken by the details of our life.

Sarah aged out of the infant program in Collin County, but she transitioned into the Plano Preschool Program for Children with Disabilities at our nearby elementary school. The assessment for entering was extensive. This was the first time I referred to Sarah as mentally retarded. It was a moment of forced acceptance, and it led to a brief spiral downward.

My moods were definitely becoming a problem.

After Sarah's birth, Michael once described me as having been in a car accident, but all the damage was internal. I wasn't the same person. My primary care doctor prescribed an anti-depressant, but I was allergic to it. A counselor diagnosed me with depression, but she also suggested I suffered from episodes of Post-Traumatic Stress Disorder and adrenal fatigue. I felt guilty and ashamed that I couldn't handle what life had thrown my way.

In truth, life wasn't all doom and gloom. We experienced laughter and joy along with our tears. We made up songs for Sarah and held her up, dancing around the house. Watching her work so hard to roll over, to crawl, and to move in her walker inspired us.

Sarah was and still is the strongest and happiest little person I've ever known.

But Michael and I were having a tough time. We were both exhausted. While we were ecstatic that Sarah was making so much progress, albeit on a significantly delayed timeline, we were under water. Anxiety and mental fatigue drained Michael's energy. And he could see the disengagement in my eyes. I was mentally checking out. We weren't communicating well, and our time together felt strained; we were alone together.

In 2000, Michael was offered a position back in the Austin area, and looking for a change in scenery, we decided to move there. Sarah originally started school attendance in a wheelchair, but through physical therapy and pure will, Sarah began walking at the age of six. Occasionally, there was a giddy-up in her step and a squeal of delight. One of my most joyful days ever was the first day I walked her to class.

Teachers and students lined the halls, and I could barely see through all my tears!

But depression continued to stalk me. After talking with my physician, I overcame my shame about the stigma of taking anti-depressants and anti-anxiety medications and finally discovered a medication that didn't give me an allergic reaction. The benefits of medication greatly improved my ability to function as I was finally able to take on each day with a better attitude.

Up until October of 2003, we were using a diagnosis of cerebral palsy to cover Sarah's physical and intellectual issues. Her pediatric gastroenterologist, Dr. Z, strongly recommended we consult with a genetic clinician. We learned through a skin biopsy that Sarah had a chromosomal disorder called Pallister-Killian Syndrome. Now we knew that Sarah's unusual facial appearance, her low muscle tone, her severe intellectual disability, and her inability to talk all fell under this diagnosis, along with the d-hernia which had led to such dire complications at birth. Thankfully, we learned that this was not an inherited disorder. While this information was indeed valuable to know, it didn't make a difference in terms of the interventions for Sarah or her prognosis; there simply were not many documented cases in the world of her rare condition.

By 2005, we were meeting each day with whatever life had to offer. There were still many frustrations and worries, but we had a happy child who was making small strides. Michael and I both coped with depression and anxiety, although his wasn't diagnosed yet.

After Sarah came home from the hospital, I had gone back on birth control pills. There was no way we could contend with another pregnancy and child. Then a few years down the road we decided to try for another child, but we weren't successful. At one point, we discussed a vasectomy, but Michael had reservations, so we postponed action until later.

Then in October of 2005, I missed my period. I took a home pregnancy test which indicated I was indeed pregnant. I cried because I was both happy and afraid. *What if something went wrong this time, too?* I was already forty-two years old! We were both worried, yet we immediately began thinking of names for our child.

People asked us if we were going to take any of the prenatal tests that were currently available to determine fetal health problems. Of course, we were! There were too many possibilities to unequivocally say what I might do in each scenario. I was mystified by a viewpoint that rules out these tests, because no matter the circumstances, the mother had already decided that abortion wasn't an option. Women often face unforeseen dilemmas when their well-being or the viability of the pregnancy falls under the shadow of a heartbreaking diagnosis; the urgency of this desperate and potentially life-threatening circumstance is no time for legislative interference. No one should make that decision for me, nor could I imagine that it's my place or anyone else's to make that decision for anyone else.

Where Sarah was concerned, knowing ahead of time that she was going to need advanced care may have saved her life. If I hadn't been provided intervention early in my pregnancy, I might have delivered her way too early, or I might have delivered her at the hospital close to our home rather than at the one with a Level IV NICU, wasting valuable time in transport. Even though the fear of knowing that something might be wrong was paralyzing, I knew that being prepared in a high-risk age bracket could potentially be lifesaving. These tests weren't foolproof, but positive results could help prepare us, and negative results could offer some measure of peace—and they did!

We were having a baby boy! Through all the self-talk and motivations I used to force myself to get up every morning, absolutely nothing could prepare me for the pure joy and love that my precious Robby would bring me.

We looked forward to the June due date with heightened anticipation, but Robby had other plans. He gave me a terrific head butt the night before Memorial Day, and my water burst. He was on his way into the world a month early! Luckily, we were able to contact our planned caregiver for Sarah.

Because Robby arrived early and was on the small side, we stayed a few extra days with him at the hospital. Doctors were on the fence about releasing him, but they discharged him with the assurance from us that he'd see his pediatrician on Monday. I couldn't bear the thought of leaving my baby at the hospital again and reliving that long ride home.

Sarah taught us to take one day at a time to cope with adversity. Robby taught us to take pleasure in the normal milestones he achieved with such ease. It was truly bittersweet to see him do all the things babies are supposed to do at the "right times," especially knowing how hard Sarah worked to accomplish any milestones. Michael was home with us those first weeks, and thankfully my dear friend Glenda came to help me later.

A new light had come into my life! When I fell in love with Michael, I didn't see how I had room in my heart to love someone else so completely. Then Sarah changed my life, and my ability to love grew. Robby was the icing on the cake. He needed me in a different way than Sarah or Michael. For the first time, when I heard the word "Momma" from his lips, I felt an even deeper love. Mingled with the challenges and heartaches of raising Sarah, we now experienced the challenges and successes of raising Robby.

Despite being stressed, exhausted, and emotional, we had hope. We sang and laughed more. And when Robby started talking, I discovered his amazing mind. He reawakened in me a sense of wonder that I hadn't felt in such a long time. I wanted to share the wonder of nature and the wonder of books and learning. We spent time together outdoors—walking the trails, climbing rocks, throwing a ball. We often read together. When he read to me, I felt such an intense fulfillment in completing this circle of shared learning.

We've experienced a great deal of joy from our two very different but remarkable children.

Having Sarah forced us to consider issues most parents will never face. For example, when Sarah approached puberty, I started a process of addressing her sexuality in light of her medical issues and her severe intellectual disability. I researched menstruation and birth control options. A partial hysterectomy seemed like the most reasonable solution. Even though she wasn't currently in situations where she was likely to be sexually assaulted, because she was disabled, the longer she survived, the greater was her risk. The local medical ethics board put up roadblocks, but with the help of an OB/GYN in another city, we were able to schedule the procedure she needed to rectify heavy bleeding and to secure permanent birth control.

We also kept an updated will because we had Sarah's needs, and later, Robby's to consider. When Sarah turned eighteen, we completed the full guardianship process to ensure Michael and I could continue making legal and medical decisions for her. We also named family members to take over guardianship of both Sarah and Robby if something were to happen to us. I also created a letter of intent to characterize how we want someone else to care for Sarah once Michael and I are gone or unable to care for her.

Sarah is now twenty-five years old, and the road ahead is still a rocky one. She completed her last school year in May 2019, which meant most of her social interaction ceased. In 2020, the year of the Covid pandemic, the infection restrictions further limited her ability to socialize with others in Special Olympics and Miracle League. Also in 2020, Sarah's doctors diagnosed her with a seizure disorder. We thought we'd dodged a bullet with seizures, but her diagnoses of PKS, autism, and hypoxia made seizures very likely.

With Michael now retired, we thankfully share more of the caregiving for both of our children. This increased time together has allowed us to talk more and to heal our relationship. Through communication and patience, our love for one another has grown.

We continue to struggle with some serious unanswered questions about Sarah's future. *Where will she live, and who will take care of her? How will both she and Robby be impacted by her future?* Services for the disabled are severely lacking in this country, particularly in Texas. Waiting lists for services for the disabled in Texas can often range from eight to twenty years depending on the type of services needed. I'm in the beginning stages of establishing a personal network for Sarah. Comprised of her family, friends, case managers, and physicians, our network will meet three or four times each year to discuss ideas to improve her life and plans for her future care. Having an entity like this network in place would benefit Sarah and would help Robby with whatever role he wants to play in caring for his sister in the future.

~~~

When considering what enabled me to cope with the challenges of life with a severely intellectually disabled daughter, some of the words that come to mind are creativity, connection, mentoring, advocacy, gratitude, and love. My unique sense of humor has also seen me through some tedious and bleak days.

Years ago, a good friend and neighbor, Cheryl, taught me how to cross stitch and also encouraged me to garden. I loved searching for designs, picking out fabrics and threads, and then getting lost in the project for long stretches of time. It was something I could do while

Sarah was at school or playing in the living room where I worked. With gardening, I spent hours outdoors doing positive physical exertion. Watching my oxblood lilies grow and bloom did me such good. Both activities gave me a way to immerse myself in something other than caregiving and to provide healing time.

After Robby came along, photography gave me a creative outlet that enabled me to document some of the wonder of the special moments we shared. Seeing the world through a camera lens helped me capture the beauty of life and gave me a more positive outlook. Creating the story of our lives in photo books gave me a deeper appreciation for what we've withstood and how we've formed a deep family connection.

Simply being outdoors was a welcome respite, whether I carried a camera in my hand or not. The restorative qualities of immersing myself in the fresh air of a forest breathing around me, the rich amber and crimson of shimmering autumn leaves, the nascent greenery of early spring, or the trickling sound of water in a creek gave me an appreciation for creation, filled me with gratitude, and healed my heart.

Connection to others has also benefited my mood and my outlook on life. It's also been the hardest aspect for me to maintain. When I give myself permission to interact with others, I usually feel renewed. A simple conversation with a friend or my sister can help swing a down mood into one that lifts me from loneliness.

Another way of connecting involved acting as a mentor and advocate. I played the role of classroom mom for Sarah's class and Special Education Parent Advisory Committee representative for the elementary school. Involvement in advocating for Sarah and for other children and their parents made me feel good about myself. Volunteering with Robby's classes added pleasure and satisfaction.

Now that I'm further along the special needs path, I offer guidance to other parents regarding transition from school to young adulthood. I gave a presentation at the Region 13 Education Service Center during a summer workshop on the importance of parents writing a Letter of Intent for their child. Keeping information together in one document about your child's medical history, personal needs, your wishes for what kind of life you envision for them, what a typical day in their life is like, their behaviors, and contact information for doctors, counselors, and community and financial resources they use can be helpful when transitioning from one guardian or caretaker to another.

Life with Sarah motivated me to become an advocate, someone who can speak up or act out. To secure what's best for my children and my community energized me to seek medical intervention from doctors, extended-year services from school administrators, or supportive action for nationwide or statewide healthcare reforms. Even with Sarah's obvious needs, I had to assert myself with doctors, especially when she needed intervention for birth control.

At the Women's March in 2017, with a few good friends I stood in support of equality and human rights. Sarah and Robby even joined me at the offices of our senators to deliver letters regarding concern about attempts to repeal the Affordable Care Act. I saw how easily medical expenses could devastate the lives of those with poor insurance or none at all and realized that healthcare was a right, not a privilege. Marching for gun regulation reform with the sign, "Books Not Bullets," and writing and mailing postcards in support of candidates for local offices kept me involved in social issues that were important to me. I continue to participate in an enlightening group, "Why Are They So Angry?", where we discuss systemic racism—its history and ongoing presence in our society—and how we can take action. My experiences have sparked an awareness of the need for compassion and action.

This awareness has enabled me to recognize how much I'm grateful for. When sharing experiences with other parents of special needs children, I see how their unique challenges affect them. I often realize that I couldn't manage what they do. Each day I see Sarah's silver lining—her happy disposition; I see Robby's special gifts—his compassion, his beautiful mind, and his sense of loyalty; I see Michael's patience, generosity, and understanding. I don't know why I'm blessed, but I know that I am.

The gifted and compassionate people who came into our lives because of Sarah's needs have filled my life with gratitude. This gratitude has spread and has effected change in many who have crossed my path.

Sarah's physical therapist at Medical City Hospital once told me, "I've learned so much from you—how to be a mother, what a family is."

Hannah, Sarah's buddy from Miracle League simply said, "You've changed my life."

I used to open my eyes in the morning feeling disillusioned by the belief that life was "normal," that I would throw my legs over the side of the bed and start a day with a "normal" child, and all would be well, only to realize that I must start a tube-feeding, change a diaper on a seven year old, or give Sarah a breathing treatment. *This* was my normal, even though it wasn't what I had hoped for. There were times when depression and anxiety medications kept my moods even; along with the extraordinary lows, I also lost the exceptional highs. Not feeling deep emotions from both ranges took conscious effort and well-balanced medications, but the payoff was knowing gratitude and providing a channel for active love.

Today, I have several goals in mind—to keep my family safe, to give them hope and laughter, and to let them feel love. Most days, I think I succeed. I hope they forgive me for the days I don't. I hope they understand that we're all somehow striving to reach a place of peace and love.

What has gotten me through this journey? My faith in people— Michael, Sarah, and Robby, mainly, but also my family, friends, teachers, and doctors. As skeptical of human nature as I've become in these divisive times, and as irreligious as I've grown to be, I still find hope in humanity. I now know love is at the heart of all of it—the connection, the gratitude, my bond with Sarah, my resilience.

Love is most nearly itself when here and now cease to matter.

—T.S. Eliot

IN THE LIGHT OF THE MOON

LAYLA SHAH

I have always believed, and still believe, that whatever good or bad fortune may come our way, we can always give it meaning and transform it into something of value.

—Hermann Hesse, *Siddhartha*

Throughout my life, I've sought light—maybe because I was born amidst so much darkness. As a child, I would always know when the moon was full. Then I would open the bedroom curtains and bask in its brightness. I loved how the moon gave its light without asking for anything in return. In Chicago's bleak winters, the face of the moon lit the snowy streets with a silvery glow.

I know the moon doesn't have its own light, but when it appears from behind the earth, it reflects the light of the sun. I've seen myself in a similar way as I try to reflect rays of light from my inner spirit. Whether it is through writing poetry or writing in my journal, writing has helped me define my voice and purpose. Through the chaos of my dysfunctional childhood, writing was a magical alchemy that turned my fears and confusion into clarity, faith, and strength. I needed that strength every day to deal with my parents and to take care of my younger brother, Wali. My parents were failing in their roles, so I had to step up. Paradoxically, I now realize that my mother's chutzpah and my father's spirituality helped me to recognize and then exit from the vicious cycles of abuse.

~~~

I grew up in a dysfunctional alcoholic household in Chicago, Illinois. One of my earliest childhood memories was of my mom pulling my two-year-old brother, Wali, and me, just a six-year-old, out of bed at 10 p.m. on a school night, throwing our thick parkas over our PJs, and walking us to a nearby neighborhood bar to search for my dad. I still remember the stench of beer and cigarettes as we stood by the blaring jukebox in the dirty bar. Old, bearded men nursing their drinks stared at us, and I was scared. Within a few minutes, mom had my dad by the arm, and she helped him stumble down the street as we all made our way back home. I didn't know about his alcoholism yet, but I was relieved to see my daddy and smell his leather coat mixed with the scent of menthol cigarettes and whiskey. His eyes and smile did not radiate their normal warmth.

After we got home, my parents started fighting. I quickly took Wali to our bedroom and tried to go to sleep. They argued for a long time until I eventually fell into a worried rest. This pattern of his drinking repeated itself regularly. Each time, I wondered what was going to happen to my family. I decided then that through prayer and self-determination, I would live a life of happiness and light, rather than one of sadness and despair.

~

It was during a blustery winter a year later that Wali and I both came down with a terrible case of the flu. He was so dehydrated that he ended up going to St. Francis Hospital in Evanston where my mother stayed with him. During the two weeks that he was there, my dad was the sole parent. At times, the experience was scary. While driving to and from the hospital, Daddy would take swigs of vodka while I sat in the back seat buckled up, trying to feel safe.

One day I said, "Daddy, it's not safe to drink and drive. You shouldn't do that. I thought you said you weren't going to drink anymore."

With a charming smile, Daddy replied, "*Beta* (his affectionate term for me in Urdu), that wasn't alcohol. Trust me, okay?" He flashed his Omar Sharif smile, and I just couldn't argue with him.

We were all deeply worried about Wali, and during one visit to the hospital, we went into the beautiful chapel to pray for my brother's recovery. I had never been inside a church, mosque, or temple as neither of my parents practiced their religions. But my father, as a Muslim from Pakistan, and my mother, as a Jew from the Northside of Chicago, occasionally had provided me with the traditions and wisdom of both cultures.

Kneeling beside my father on the wooden row of benches closest to the door I asked, "Daddy, aren't you a Muslim, and isn't Mom Jewish? Why are we here?" My father smiled at me and whispered back, "God has no religion. It doesn't matter where you pray or what religion you are. God will hear you if it comes from your heart." When my dad closed his eyes in prayer, so did I. For several minutes, we were both silent in prayer for Wali's recovery.

After spending two weeks in the hospital, we were all relieved when Wali was allowed to return home. I have never forgotten that experience with my father. From it I learned that if your heart is open to it, the presence of God can be felt in any place of worship. Yes, God exists everywhere. The Sufi poet Rumi's words echoed this truth when he wrote, "I looked in temples, churches, and mosques. But I found the Divine within my heart." My father was an alcoholic, yet I learned some of my most foundational spiritual truths from him; sometimes our greatest heroes are deeply tormented and flawed people who also possess important positive qualities.

As the years passed, my brother and I often waited anxiously for my dad to come home from work as my mother's mental health was deteriorating under the pressure of my father's alcoholism and her own inner demons.

One cold January day, we woke to find Mom angry and mumbling in her bedroom. She told me, "Go back to sleep and wake up later." I obeyed her but was afraid and stared at the ceiling for a long time. Finally, I heard Wali giggling. I followed the joyful but naughty sound to our living room. He had the TV on and was watching *He-Man*. Soon, Mom came in with our favorite breakfast, cinnamon toast— even though it was past noon. That day we were even allowed to eat in the living room while watching TV, which was rare.

We started playing around, and Wali got up and swung his toy rifle. Before I knew it, he had accidentally swung it towards the coffee table. The heavy rifle fell from his hands and broke a large crystal bowl.

"You *mamzer*, you!" screamed our infuriated mother. "Which one of you bastards did this? You think this is funny?"

Wali's eyes were wide with fear as he began to cry. I knew my brother was too young to face Mom's wrath alone. When I stood up for Wali, I found myself in a world of trouble. Mom quickly grabbed my Barbie doll bed and broke it over her knees. My brother started to defend me, but I told him not to. Deep within, I silently prayed a combination of Arabic prayers I had learned from my paternal relatives mixed with my own prayers in English. These prayers helped me to remain mentally and emotionally strong.

Over the years, to lighten the somber mood of our house, Wali and I made each other laugh by making fun of Mom behind her back. At the time, we didn't realize she carried such a heavy burden as she took care of us when my father was out late drinking and irresponsibly handling money. We feared her temper, so we tried to find acceptance outside our house. It was many years before I realized that in spite of her problems, it was my mother who fed us, clothed us, and made sure we got to school daily.

~~~

When I was seventeen, on a rare quiet night at our apartment, disaster struck. Mom, Wali, and I waited till about 10:30 p.m. for Dad to get home. We all knew he must have been drinking as this was way too late for him to be at work. We all had seen the red flags. Despite the DWI's piling up, he was still drinking. At 11:45 p.m., I was drifting off to sleep and feeling the burdens of the day lift when the phone rang. I woke up, knowing by the pain in my heart that this phone call would have something to do with Dad's drinking.

That night, while my mother and brother stayed home, my uncle and I bailed my father out of jail for public intoxication. I contributed $500 from my car savings account that I had earned from a part-time job. It turned out my father had gotten into an argument with a man at the bar who was wearing a "Fly 5,000 Miles Just to Smoke a Camel" shirt at the height of the Iraq War. So in my drunken dad's wild eyes, an absurd t-shirt justified starting an altercation. The court ordered my dad to attend AA meetings.

When I was eighteen, my dad finally stopped drinking. At first, he was cynical about attending AA meetings, but over time, he started getting help from his Higher Power and became sober. For a few years, I would often accompany him to the meetings, drinking coffee and quietly listening to everyone's recovery stories. I came to admire the strength and beauty of people who could admit their wrongs, commit to self-improvement, and gather to support each other in their quests for recovery. It was a gift to my father that instead of hating him for his years of alcoholism, I finally understood he had a disease that he was committed to heal.

Nonetheless, despite my father's recovery, my parents' trauma affected me. People-pleasing behavior is often attributed to trauma, especially the trauma caused from having an alcoholic parent. For many years, I found myself in situations where I bent over backwards to be seen as a good person, to be valued, and to be accepted. Since my alcoholic father and traumatized mother were always the center of attention, I felt invisible. I struggled to be seen.

When I left home at eighteen and lived with my best friend Persephone, my life became more about attending college classes, spending time with my friends, and developing myself through writing and reading. During those early years of living away from my parents, I learned that life did not have to be full of drama or instability. I also learned that I could create a peaceful life for myself.

But poor Wali was left to live with my parents. He eventually joined a local gang, and after seeing a friend get shot, he suffered from schizophrenia induced by his PTSD. Today, he is a grown man who still lives at home with my parents. It's a heartbreaking situation as my parents have thwarted my efforts to help him.

～～

I met my first husband, Adan, when I was working at a Montessori school in Denton, Texas. I was his daughter's preschool teacher, and he was divorced from her mother. I didn't know it at the time, but like my father, he was an alcoholic. Our marriage only lasted six years, and during those years he was often out of town working in oil production, or so he said. I divorced him when I found out that for many months, he had been having an affair with a stripper.

We had just moved to Laredo, Texas, from Liberty, Pennsylvania, and our son, Sebastian, was three years old at the time. I had entered Texas A&M International University and was ready for a fresh start.

One night, Adan came home from working in the oil fields at 2:00 a.m. and went straight to bed. He stank of liquor and plopped down on the bed without taking his clothes off, barely saying a word to me. I went back to bed, unsure what was going on.

As I was drifting off to sleep, I heard banging on the front door. When I got up, I found a wailing woman at our door. I later learned that she was the woman from the local strip joint Adan had been seeing when he had told me he was working late. When I would ask him if there was any other reason that he was so late, he would just accuse me of being jealous or crazy. Closer to our actual divorce, Adan admitted that his alcoholic binges had ruined his life. He didn't take actions to rectify this situation, so I decided not to be the bitter wife of an alcoholic like my mother was for so many years. An individual suffering from alcoholism needs to admit to the problem and then find help for it. As I learned from my childhood, it takes some people many years before they accept their situation or ask for help.

After months of trying to work through our relationship in counseling, I finally left Adan. Our son Sebastian was only four years old. I was still in college, as I had returned to school at thirty-one; I knew I had to complete my college degree if I was to have a successful future. So as a single mom, I finished my BA in English at Texas A&M International University. As difficult as those years were, my love for my son fueled me to keep going and to achieve some goals I had never actualized before, like earning a 3.7 GPA and securing a part-time job at the local newspaper as a writer and editor. I learned self-discipline during those challenging years as a student because I was working part-time and raising my son. Even through the crazy drama with Adan, I kept

going to school and focusing on what was most important to me—
raising my son Sebastian and continuing my education.

~~~

After being divorced for three years and finishing my BA, I met
my second husband, Emanuel, at a local mosque. My friends and I had
created a university group called Operation Feed the Homeless. I was
working hard to get the Muslim community involved, and Emanuel
joined us several times. He befriended me, and we eventually started to
date. I quickly thought he would be the love of my life because we had
so many shared interests, and he seemed like such a caring individual.
It was a whirlwind romance as we were married within a year. We had
a beautiful wedding that my best friend hosted at her home in Dallas and then we honeymooned in Spain. Sebastian adored Emanuel,
so that sealed our partnership even more tightly. All the hard work,
prayer, and positive energy I had been putting into Sebastian's and my
life seemed to be paying off.

But even before we married, Emanuel's hot temper and unhealthy
habits were beginning to peek out as little red flags marring our oth-
erwise idyllic relationship. By the first year of our marriage, his fits of
rage were taking a toll on our relationship, creating a negative pattern
in our house. He sought some help, but it was never consistent.

When we had our son Omar almost a year after we married,
Emanuel's insomnia and mood swings reminded me so much of the
dysfunctional house of my childhood. He argued with me whenever I
brought up the inequality in our relationship. When I pointed out that

I was doing more than my fair share of chores in the house and that his behavior was erratic and antisocial, he said, "You disrespect me daily!"

At the time, I was also in graduate school and working full time as a teacher. However, I still was the only one who got up to calm our colicky baby at night. I was a depressed, walking zombie after staying up most of the night and then working all day. Emanuel decided to sleep on the sofa to not be disturbed from his sleep. Yes, there were times he occasionally helped me, but our partnership was far from equal. I worked full time, took graduate school classes, and cared for our newborn son in addition to raising Sebastian who was nine years old at the time.

Years passed, and our relationship suffered even more. Our son Omar was two years old when Emanuel's anger outbursts became more frequent and his behavior more unpredictable.

I finally realized that neither my children nor I needed to be exposed to his explosive behavior. A few days later, I took out a loan and hired a lawyer to file for a divorce. But then Emanuel promised to change.

The months passed, and his behavior didn't change, so I filed for a divorce again. This time, there was nothing he could say that would change my mind.

When I divorced my first husband, Adan, I was a timid undergrad with a four-year-old son. Over time, I became a graduate student and a confident single mother. This time around, I was a woman with a master's degree and a stable teaching job.

A month before our divorce was finalized and a few days after I moved into a new apartment, I was feeling the deep pains of missing

Omar as due to our shared custody agreement, he often lived with Emanuel.

That night my father surprised me with a phone call.

"*Beta*, please don't think I don't know what you're going through. You are incredible, and I am proud of you. The entire *khandaan*, our family, is proud of you."

"Really, Dad? This sure is a revelation to me. I have always felt like a black sheep in our family."

"Layla, I have to tell you what your aunt, *Seema phooppoo*, said the last time you visited. She was in the room talking to me about how much you're just like her. As you know, she also was a highly educated woman living with two sons and an emotionally abusive husband. Now she is finally divorced, happy, and successful. She said everyone in the family adores you and respects your strength. I'm so proud of you."

"Well, thank you, dad. I hadn't thought the family accepted me, let alone respected me. But I had thought about how I am uncannily like *Seema phoopoo*. "

It was rare that a divorced woman would be accepted in a paternal Pakistani Muslim family. It was even more rare to receive any kind of praise from my father, because in general, South Asian fathers are not very emotive.

Yet I couldn't help but finally feel understood. But I still wondered, would I remain single the rest of my life like *Naseema phoopoo*, my father's older sister?

I also thought of my mother's only sister, Shelley, who I was very close to. Aunt Shelley was a single mother at a young age and a fabulous painter who eventually found the love of her life in middle age. Though she passed away several years ago, her sparkling personality and persistent character still inspire me. Would I follow her path?

Since my sons and I left my second abusive marriage, I've found an increased passion for life.

After moving to our new apartment, I had a very lucid dream. In the dream I was in our new living room where I saw a large dreidel, a Jewish spinning top used for Hanukkah. It had colorful writing engraved on it, but I couldn't decipher what it said.

When I woke the next morning, I remembered my dream and looked at the Hebrew letters on our family's dreidel. In English, the words translate as *A Great Miracle Happened Here*. Maybe it was a message from my subconscious mind or a Divine intervention. Today, I know that a great miracle is taking place as I embark on a peaceful new life with my boys in our new apartment. Each day I try to lead by example and continue balancing my life as a loving mom, an inspiring English teacher, and an accomplished writer.

Unfortunately, right after I moved, Omar was diagnosed with autism spectrum disorder. Omar is now in kindergarten, and as we await his IEP (Individualized Education Program), he has had a bumpy start getting used to his new, more-disciplined environment. I have found grace as Emanuel and I have learned to be amicable for the sake of

Omar. We advocate for him at his school meetings, including his ARD (Admission, Review, and Dismissal) meetings, and I consider us on the same team to help our son be the bright shining star we know he is meant to be. I know that I am doing the brunt of the paper and leg work, but I feel blessed to be able to do this for him. While I now have definite boundaries with Emanuel, I am also free of anger in my dealings with him—what a blessing this is!

Often the lessons we don't learn in life come back to haunt us. For me, it's to pay attention to red flags in relationships, to set firm boundaries, and to respect myself. Just as the moon waxes and wanes, becomes full and then crescents again, sometimes we feel less light, and other times we feel the light fully.

But this is a new phase of the moon. I'm proud of myself for once again realizing that after years of chaos and fighting, I'm climbing out of the dark hole so that I could see the moon again. I'm realizing that love is not enough to sustain a relationship. Occasional abuse is still abuse, and what we often write off as arguments or frequent bad moods is still emotional abuse. When you don't know when a person will fly off the handle, you constantly walk around on eggshells trying to keep the peace. This isn't a way to live.

I'm now showing my boys that when you give someone your heart, you deserve respect and lasting love. It should be a love that you do not doubt or see only on special occasions. I've decided to make sure that the ugly past will have no power over me in the future as I build a life for me and my sons. We don't have to just survive; we must thrive.

I've learned that if you leave an abusive relationship that brings toxicity into your life, you have already won—even if you are lonely or worry about the financial strain or the social stigma of divorce. Self-love and peace are priceless and are valuable gifts you can pass on to your children. Also, knowing who you are—no matter how others try to define you—will keep you centered on your goals rather than on trying to prove something to someone else.

I've also learned that the best gift we can give our children is our unconditional love. While our family's financial status has changed and our home and family are now smaller, we still have a home, and we are still a loving family. Things have been lost; however, peace, hope, and a new sense of purpose have been won. Through it all, I have never stopped loving and encouraging my sons to be the best that they can be. Together, we are now reaching for the stars.

~~~~

Have you ever felt like your past has prepared you for your current life? From an early age I learned that in the darkness I must find the moonlight to illuminate my path. Often, I've forgotten to brighten my own path while lighting the way for others. Again and again, I've been reminded that we must be the heroes of our own stories; even if others help me, the decisive action that works best is often my own consistent positive behavior. I, just as much as anyone else, deserve my love and compassion.

Sometimes we paradoxically find the very things we thought we lost on our journeys. While mourning the loss of my marriages, I discovered that the love of my two children and my self-love is the love that I was always searching for. And it took my dreaded second divorce to circle back to the realization that everything that happened, even the painful parts, has made me into an improved version of myself. I've picked up the pieces of my past to build new dreams for the future. I am now the full light of the moon for both myself and my children as I guide them to finding their own inner light.

CENTERED AFTER ALL

JAN QUESADA

"Are you alone?"

I was in Fort Worth just beginning my drive home to Dallas after a day of teaching. I have a dream job teaching Religion and Biblical Studies to undergraduates at Texas Christian University. When I received the phone call from my general practitioner and heard her first question, I was in fact alone in my Subaru. As I sat at a traffic light and waited to merge onto the highway, Dr. N. informed me, "The MRI mammogram from last week shows a blurry spot in your left breast."

While I recognized that her opening question cast an ominous shadow over her news, I felt more annoyed than frightened. In my view, this medical result foretold a series of inconvenient medical tests in the middle of the semester. I did regular self-exams and had never felt a lump.

Over the years, I had been called back for numerous follow-up mammograms due to radiologists being concerned about seeming anomalies in my dense breast tissue. Until this moment, all of those previous tests had raised only false alarms.

This call, however, would mark the beginning of my year-long odyssey with breast cancer.

I should not have been surprised. Breast cancer runs in my family. My mother was diagnosed with breast cancer and had her first mastectomy at age forty-nine. After numerous mammogram scares, she had her second breast removed twenty years later. Thankfully, now well into her eighties, she continues to live a rich and full life today.

Her mother, my beloved grandmother, had an aggressive form of breast cancer that took her life within a year when she was eighty-four. My mother's older and only sister, Aunt Marilyn, died from metastatic breast cancer at age sixty-four, and her daughter, my cousin Melinda, was diagnosed with breast cancer at age fifty-seven, my exact age.

I had told my gynecologist, Dr. R., about the alarming history of breast cancer on the maternal side of my family, and she had kept an eye on my annual mammograms. But when I turned fifty-six, she administered a "My Risk" blood test to determine, as the name suggests, my likelihood of getting breast cancer. When the results came back, my lifetime risk was assessed to be 20.1 percent. This assessment, my gynecologist informed me, just barely met the minimum standard of "more than 20 percent" when insurance companies would pay for a baseline MRI mammogram. So, at her urging, I scheduled an MRI mammogram in February of 2020.

I credit this doctor, Dr. R., with saving my life.

It was my first MRI. The headphones the technician gave me played the mellow James Taylor ballads I had requested to buffer the metallic banging of the machine, and the scan was soon completed. I didn't give it much thought after I dressed and headed home. *It's just a baseline test*, I reassured myself. And then I received that phone call several days later from my primary care doctor. When she informed me of the blurred spot, I channeled my worry into busyness. I focused on putting the final touches on a regional religious studies conference I was organizing in early March. "Denial is not just a river in Egypt," the wise pun goes.

I needed a sonogram to try to generate a better image of the area. I had had many sonograms before—mainly as a part of the prenatal care I received during my four pregnancies. By this time in my life, I had four wonderful adult children, two sons and two daughters ranging in ages from eighteen to thirty. I associated sonograms with getting to look at a screen and seeing black and white images of my gestating babies.

This appointment was different; it hurt. The technician was diligent in rubbing the sonogram wand deeply into the breast tissue for what seemed like a very long time as she tried to get a satisfactory image. Finally, she left the darkened room and came back with a radiologist.

"We weren't able to get a good image of the area," he informed me. "You'll need to speak to your doctor about next steps." I could tell from his tone that this was not good news, but I still refused to accept the problem. *If they couldn't image it, and I couldn't feel it, then it must be nothing.*

According to the medical protocol in this situation, my gynecologist recommended an MRI-guided needle biopsy. I was skeptical and dismayed. I complained to my husband Tex, "I can't feel any sort of a lump, the sonogram couldn't find it, and I don't want to have another test, especially not such an invasive one." He listened patiently, and then he asked, "What do you have to lose?"

"Money, for one thing," I said. "This test will be expensive."

"Why leave the question hanging? And it's only money. Just do it," he said. "Let's not look back and have any regrets."

He had a point.

By this time, it was mid-March of 2020, and my regional conference for 260 religion scholars and students was over. It had been a satisfying success. We had managed to host it just days before Covid ballooned into a scary and disruptive presence in Dallas, in Texas, in the United States, and in the world. My university, TCU, extended spring break by a week and told its faculty to prepare to teach the remaining weeks of the semester in an online format. Faculty and students in all sorts of schools were facing daunting challenges.

Our younger son, a senior in high school, had to navigate the last three months of his senior year on Zoom. Capstone events like his prom and senior days were cancelled altogether. Even graduation would have to be online.

Tex and his law partners were trying to figure out how to shift their practice to a remote format. Worship services for our church were moved to live-stream. Fear and uncertainty were pervasive, as we, like so many, tried to evade this spooky new disease by masking up, wiping down the groceries we had ordered online, and staying home as much as possible.

Meanwhile, I had followed my husband's advice and scheduled the biopsy. On a Thursday morning, he drove me to the imaging center but couldn't come inside, thanks to Covid protocols. I went in alone—masked up and socially distanced—not knowing what to expect. The nurse found me after I had changed out of my street clothes.

"Here is your Xanax." She held out a tiny paper cup with the pill in it.

"What is it for?"

"To help you stay relaxed during the procedure," she said.

"May I take a half dose?" I asked.

"If you'd like," she shrugged.

I hadn't yet spoken to my mother about any of these tests, knowing that she became distraught each time I needed a follow-up mammogram. She viewed the possibility of my getting breast cancer somehow as her fault. I would need to phone her after the biopsy, and I wanted to be able to speak with her coherently. The nurse returned with half a pill which I swallowed, hoping that it would do the trick. I wasn't thinking clearly about the "needle" part of the "MRI-guided needle biopsy."

Isolated and draped in a hospital gown, I waited for the half Xanax to take effect. I sat in a recliner in a small room off the main corridor. A curtain was pulled partway across the doorway. I glanced up as another patient, a lovely blonde who looked to be in her mid-thirties, paused, looked directly at me, and said, "I'm praying for you."

"I'm praying for you, too," I replied. *What had just happened? I had never seen this woman before, nor did she know me. Yet, this fellow patient had stopped to encourage me. Like a Divine messenger, she gifted me with the assurance of her prayers.* This moment is now etched in my memories of that fateful day, and another sign that I was not alone.

The biopsy was the most painful part of my entire breast cancer experience. Why didn't I take the recommended dose of the anti-anxiety drug? The words *medieval* and *torture* come to mind.

Two hours after I had entered the building, I climbed back into Tex's car.

"How did it go?" he asked as he pulled out of the parking lot.

I turned to him with a grimace.

"That was awful. Please take me home so I can phone Mom and then go to sleep." I had been told to expect a call with a biopsy report from Dr. R. on Monday.

By the next day, and for several weeks after, my left breast turned an ugly dark purple from the bruising and bleeding this test had caused. "My poor little breast," as I called it, was a piteous sight.

⌣⌣⌣

With the extended spring break ending and so much still to do to prepare for online teaching, and with Tex's office going into remote mode, we decided to drive to our ranch. Located two-hundred miles west of Dallas in a broad, shallow canyon surrounded by mesas and farms, the ranch is our oasis. There is a small rock house with a big front porch that was there when we bought it. We built a larger stone house in 2016 that is surrounded by cedar, prickly pear, and mesquite. This newer house became our lock-down sanctuary. Tex worked from its detached office space, while I improvised a desk on the kitchen countertop. Our ranch was the perfect place to escape to during the pandemic.

On Friday, after provisioning our Dallas house for our eighteen-year-old son, we packed up our old shepherd mix mutt, Ginger, and headed west. Jane and Mike, our good friends, were already at the ranch settled into the small rock house that they now owned. With no idea what lay ahead or how long the pandemic might last, we decided to become a "pod" for its duration.

Over the weekend, I prepared for the next week's classes by embedding mini audio lectures into a PowerPoint on biblical prophets. I took some long reflective walks along the dusty caliche roads and rocky trails. Jane and I worked on a 1000-piece jigsaw puzzle of a Renoir landscape that diverted us for hours. She and I also took turns cooking dinners, and we all watched the Michael Jordan documentary, *The Last Dance*, in lieu of the Covid-cancelled NCAA basketball tournament.

Monday passed in a haze of activity as I evaluated seventy student email assignments and replied to each of them individually from 10 a.m. until 6 p.m. There were still no phone calls from the doctor. On Tuesday morning, I contacted her office to check on the report.

"Dr. R. is out of the office today," the receptionist said.

"I'm waiting on a test result that was supposed to be ready yesterday," I explained.

"I will have her call you soon," she assured me.

At 12:30, my cell phone rang.

"Is this a good time to talk?" Dr. R. asked. "I'm sorry for the delay. I have your biopsy report, but I have been at my lake house with guests and needed to wait to call you until after they left."

I knew then that the news would not be good. "Let me get something to write with," I said. Then, I took a deep breath, released it slowly, and listened.

"The biopsy revealed a cancerous growth in your left breast. It's a DCIS—a ductal carcinoma in situ," she said. The terminology was new to me, and I asked that she repeat it. DCIS is a type of breast cancer that is in an early stage and is located within a milk duct.

"This is relatively good news, I guess?"

"Yes, but I still don't have the complete report which will indicate its hormone sensitivity and growth rate."

"What should I do now?" I asked.

She gave me the names of a couple of specialists and breast cancer surgeons in Dallas and said that I should call one of them and schedule an appointment. "If my mother or sister had what you have," she said, "I would refer them to one of these physicians."

I said goodbye, trusting that she had guided me toward skilled cancer specialists.

Cancer. The word itself was ominous. Latching onto the one element of good news, I found Tex in his office, and blurted out, "It turns out that I do have breast cancer, but they've caught it early."

He looked at me first with alarm, and then with loving concern. After hugging me tight for a long moment, he pulled back and asked, "What's next?"

I got to work and called a specialist's office. Due to the high rates of Covid hospitalizations, the Texas governor had announced *the day before* a moratorium on all elective surgeries. Consequently, when I called the surgeon's office, she had numerous openings to see me soon.

After an early dinner with Jane and Mike, Tex and I headed back to Dallas. The drive was punctuated by our phone calls to our three older children and my mother. The news still felt slightly unreal.

Our older son, Ross, wanted to help me find a flight to another state where I could get more immediate access to surgery and promised us half of his stash of N-95 masks—they were still so hard to find. My daughter Brooke told me that she would be willing to come to Dallas from Los Angeles to take care of me during my treatments. She had just begun a new printing and book-binding business when Covid struck, yet she was willing to put it all aside for me. I was amazed and humbled by her offer. When we got home, we shared the news with our son Samuel. He looked at me with kindness in his brown eyes and hugged me.

"Just remember," he said, "you have the most survivable form of cancer. You're gonna be okay."

I absorbed this hopeful perspective and held fast to his words. "I'm gonna be okay," I repeated silently. "May it be so," I said.

The next morning, Tex and I drove to Presbyterian Hospital and were met outside with near-empty parking lots and inside by a screening team for the women's health center. This trio was taking temperatures and issuing fresh surgical masks. On this first medical visit, Tex was allowed to come with me. I took a "before selfie" of us that reminded me of his lovingkindness. In the image, my shaggy bangs swoop down across my forehead, and his face tilts back a bit, but we are both smiling. You can tell from our eyes that together we are determined to face whatever lay ahead.

I was not alone.

We were meeting a renowned breast cancer surgeon, Dr. G. She exuded friendliness and compassion, as well as a keen intelligence.

"What are you reading?" she asked about the book I had brought into the examining room.

When I showed her that it was Geraldine Brooks' *Year of Wonders*, set in the English countryside during the 1665 bubonic plague, Dr. G. told me she had read another book by the same author and enjoyed it. She and I clicked. I felt like I was a real person to her, not just a "case."

Dr. G. gave us a clear and succinct description, based on the full report, of the sort of cancer I had and what my treatment options would be.

Pointing to the radiology images from the MRI, she described the dimensions, location, identified its hormonal profile, and explained the two concerning elements—the cancer had made a "micro-invasion" outside the duct, and it was positive for the HER2 protein, which is a spreading agent for cancers. Surgery would be necessary, along with possible radiation treatments. Given the cancer's location, a lumpectomy would leave me with a large dimple on the lower half of my breast.

I asked about the possibility of her doing a radical (bi-lateral) mastectomy instead. I knew that my mother had opted for a mastectomy and survived her breast cancer, whereas her sister had opted for a lumpectomy and had not.

I wanted to be rid of all my breast tissue which suddenly seemed menacing. Dr. G. replied that insurance companies usually approved mastectomies as they saved them money in the long run. And having one would certainly save me worry.

For all our discussions of surgery, it could not be scheduled any time soon due to the governor's moratorium. Nevertheless, we needed to find an oncologist and a plastic surgeon. Dr. G. gave us some names for both specialties, and we left her office. Just as we were pulling out of the parking lot, her office called to say that the plastic surgeon she preferred to work with on breast reconstruction cases was in his office doing dictation. He would be happy to consult with us right then if possible. This felt like a miracle.

Dr. K's office was on the other side of the hospital campus, and this gracious man spent over an hour with us explaining the procedures and reviewing the options for reconstruction after a double mastectomy. We had a folder of information to digest once we got back home but felt confident that I would be in very good hands for what lay ahead.

As we drove back to the ranch that evening, we were both quiet, processing all we had heard that day. To fill the silence, Tex put on a playlist of some of our favorite songs. As Bob Marley crooned his reggae song "No Woman, No Cry," tears welled up in my eyes. I understood that Tex was using carefully curated music to console me during this fearful time.

For most of the three-hour drive, the music played and the lyrics washed over me, creating a residue of hope by the time we pulled into the ranch. Without speaking at all, Tex had said so much.

The next day was my fifty-seventh birthday. It was actually a really good day with numerous calls and well wishes from family and friends, most of whom were not yet aware of the "DCIS with micro-invasion" news.

Through the wonders of telemedicine, I was able to meet with the brilliant oncologist who sketched out my non-surgical treatment plan. This woman, Dr. J., managed to be both helpful and amusing as she explained the challenges of fighting cancer.

She presented this analogy: the sort of weapon that one would use against a tiger—such as a gun—would be both inappropriate and ineffective if the problem were a swarm of ants. So instead of massive doses of harsh chemo drugs, she would devise a chemo cocktail of Taxol and Herceptin, a drug which targets the HER2 protein. I would go in a week later to have a preliminary appointment at the oncology center and to get my orientation to chemotherapy.

Having a medical plan—especially without the option of an immediate surgery—lifted my spirits. I was able to relax and savor the delicious birthday dinner that Jane made for me that evening. Gratitude bubbled up as I read the messages of my birthday cards. I was loved, and I was not alone. With this gift of awareness, one year of my life ended, and another year began.

~~~

Cancer is a foreign country, and I was just beginning the journey through it. I trusted my new medical guides. I was learning the strange language, and I was connecting with fellow travelers. So many beloved women in my life—my mother, my cousin, my neighbor, and many more dear friends both old and new—had made the same harrowing journey and emerged alive and well.

The oncologist, Dr. J., had instructed me that to keep my strength and stamina during chemo, I needed to walk at least four hours each week. The ranch offered me the ideal setting for such walks—with my dog, with Jane, or solo. Usually in the morning, and often more than once a day, I put on my knee-high snake boots, a hat, and sunglasses, and set off for a restorative trek. I referred to this practice as a walking prayer or praying with my eyes open.

In life and in death, I belong to God.

This affirmation came to me early on as I walked along a red dirt ranch road, past the pond and toward the trail that led up into the hills. I passed the scrub brush surrounding a stand of shaggy oak trees. I walked on by a small wall of prickly pear cactus growing along the fence-line. As I pondered the news of my diagnosis, this phrase emerged in my mind, establishing whose I am, in this life and in the next. It became a sort of mantra for me and a source of whispered confidence for the days ahead.

I wasn't in danger of dying, but the diagnosis of cancer got my attention and helped me relocate myself in terms of my ultimate values. I was determined to orient myself "God-ward," no matter what lay ahead.

I know this to be experientially true: Prayer is powerful. Prayer carried me through my entire cancer ordeal. I am certain that I was able to navigate the challenges of the year because prayer supported, energized, and renewed me, even when I was unable to pray. I was not as frightened or as sick or as listless as I could have been. I felt that I was held in a loving and stabilizing embrace. What a luminous gift. Never doubt that prayers matter. They do.

Reading back through the journal I kept throughout the year of my cancer treatment, I see several patterns emerge.

I was understandably self-focused. I paid close attention to how I felt, what my schedule was, and what I needed to do to tend to my well-being. I needed rest. Check. I needed to take a walk. Check. I needed to hydrate and eat a nourishing meal. Check. I needed to be at my appointments on time. Check. I also keenly felt the beauty of simple daily experiences. I would walk around the southern corner of the front porch at the ranch house and let the morning sun kiss my face. I would close my eyes and savor with deep gratitude the fact that I was alive—under the sun instead of under the ground. The sweetness of that awareness could permeate the entire day.

I paid close daily attention to the living creatures and the flowering plants around me. Catching sight of the glory that is a painted bunting—a tiny bird that looks like it's been spray-painted red and yellow, blue and green—provoked my sense of wonder. I marveled at the ferocious energy of the tiny, jewel-colored hummingbirds as they swooped and buzzed each other while competing for the sugar water in our feeders. Catching sight of the small gray fox with a watermelon rind in his jaws delighted me. Seeing the fat little quail with his topknot sit on the wire fence and call in his slow and earnest two-toned song for his mate gave me such pleasure.

I was dazzled by the cactus flowers—neon yellow and brimming with pollen in the late spring. The wildflowers—Indian paintbrush, black-eyed Susans, purple thistle, bluebonnets, and all manner of daisies—astonished me with their beauty.

All my senses became more acute than before. This awakening of my senses was one of cancer's best gifts.

~~~~

As we drove back to Dallas for my first chemo treatment in mid-April, we beheld a natural world that was flourishing and fruitful. Baby calves were in the pastures; wildflowers lined the highways and farm-to-market roads; purple and white iris bloomed in yards; the leaves of the myriad mesquite trees fluttered neon apple green; and yucca plants, topped with cones of buxom white blossoms from all the heavy spring rains, adorned the whole countryside.

When I stepped out of the car at the oncology center, a child's poster taped next to the entryway greeted me. The poster featured a joyous, burly rainbow, magic markers almost spent in the young artist's lavish effort to fill the space with all the colors. Under the rainbow's purple arc was the bold message: *Everything will be OK!*

Tears sprang to my eyes. I blinked and smiled, buoyed by a jolt of hope as I walked through the automated glass doors. I thanked God for the comforting kindness of this anonymous young artist, whose message illuminated the web of compassion that links the sick with those who long for their healing.

The chemo port had been surgically implanted under the skin just below my right clavicle. It was connected to a tube that emptied into the vena cava, the largest vein in the body, just as the base of my neck. When I received a chemo infusion, the nurse would puncture the skin to connect with the port, and the fluids (saline, Benadryl, Taxol, Herceptin) would drip from the bag through the clear tubing and enter my body through the port. From there, they entered my bloodstream through the vena cava. I could never feel any of this liquid transfer as a direct sensation, but I could imagine the chemicals being flushed down the vena cava and integrated into my bloodstream, working their therapeutic magic. I would, however, feel the effects of the Benadryl.

On my second infusion day, I sat across from a lady with big hair and a Texas twang. "Oh, honey," she told me, "that Benadryl—that's just like a margarita." And it was.

I had brought Sudoku and crossword puzzles to pass the time during my first chemo appointment but was too woozy to work them after the first few minutes. In fact, most of my memories of chemo involve reclining in a comfortable spa chair, being wrapped in a blanket with fuzzy socks on my feet, and watching HGTV shows until I fell into a deep sleep. I would wake up as the nurse removed the needle from my port, put my shoes back on, fold up my blanket, and walk outside to meet Tex for the ride home.

My oncologist told me that how I felt each day of the first week after chemo would set the expectations of how the rest of my chemo experience would be. This was, mainly, true. My infusions were always set for Fridays. Tex and I would head home from the ranch on Thursday evenings and have dinner with our son. On Friday mornings, Tex would take me to the oncology center where I would check in, get my blood pressure and oxygen rate taken, weigh in, have my blood drawn into three vials, and wait to be called back to the infusion lab. Sometimes, I would meet with the nurse who generally had mental health questions for me, and other times, I would meet with the oncologist, who would examine my chest, ask encouraging questions, and tell me that things looked like they were going well. Then, I would get my infusion.

As Tex drove us back out to our ranch, I would sleep most of the way. On Saturday, I would have lots of energy, apparently from the steroids that were part of my chemo cocktail. I would clean the house and go for walks and feel good. Then, on Sunday, I would feel blah—no energy, no affect. Then, on Monday, I would feel normal again and go back to online teaching and grading. When I asked the oncology nurse about my depressive feeling on Sundays, she suggested that it was my body's reaction to coming off of the steroids and the high energy they produced. Once I understood this dynamic, I quit worrying so much about my Sunday blues.

By the third chemo treatment when I still had my hair, the oncologist said that I might not lose it. However, the next week when I washed it, my hair began coming out in large clumps. I looked down in horror at my hands, which were full of tangled clumps of wet brown hair. I waited a week. Then I asked Jane to shave my head. As I sat on the side porch of the ranch house on a bar stool with a towel placed around my shoulders, she began to cut the longer strands of my hair. I watched as they fell onto the decking and floated away in the breeze. I closed my eyes so I would not have to see all of it fall and blow away. Then, Jane began to shave my head—first in a buzz cut length, and then to smooth baldness. In the end, I looked like an honest-to-goodness cancer patient. Dammit. My cousin, who had been through her own breast cancer journey three years before me and heard about my hair loss, sent me two of her chemo wigs and an assortment of wonderful knit caps. I loved the knit caps. One was a stretchy blue turban with a paisley print, and one looked more like a dusty purple flat-top cap. They felt clean and elegant.

When I tried on the wigs, however, I looked a bit like Phyllis Diller. Cue the cigarette holder and get me some false eyelashes! Instead of a wig, I chose to wear a cap, a turban, a scarf, or to go bare-headed. Being mainly at the ranch freed me to leave my bare head bare and not worry about startling anyone. I did, however, wear a hat to bed so I wouldn't get cold.

As we sat on our sofa in our living room one quiet evening, Tex draped his arm over my shoulder.

"Did you think you'd get lucky and dodge this disease?" he asked.

"I did," I said. Based on an article I had read years ago linking breast-feeding with a lower rate of breast cancer, I thought I might avoid it. My mom, my aunt, and their mother had not been able to successfully breastfeed. I was a bottle-fed baby, as my mom had been. But I had been able to breastfeed each of my four children. I imagined that this fact was a kind of medical shield. Actually, it was a comforting fantasy, now fully punctured.

～～～

Spring turned into summer as the twelve weekly chemo sessions elapsed. By mid-June, I enjoyed a four-week reprieve with no treatments so that my body could gain strength prior to the double mastectomy surgery that was set for mid-July.

The morning of the surgery, Tex dropped me off at the hospital entrance, and I walked in alone. The check-in proceeded smoothly. I was soon lying on a gurney, with an IV needle in my hand, hospital socks on my feet, a shower cap on my bald head, and a warm white blanket draped over my body. Just before I put my cell phone away, my daughter Tessa called.

"Brooke and I are thinking of you, Mama," she said. "We hope everything goes well with your surgery. We love you!" Her voice was a cheery balm. I settled my head back on the thin pillow, relinquished the phone, and tried to pay attention as the anesthesiologist explained the sort of drugs that he would use to keep me sedated. I smiled as the gurney rolled toward the surgery and took comfort in Tessa's words as my consciousness slipped mercifully away for a while.

The plan after surgery was for me and my mom to stay at Jane and Mike's Dallas house for a week. We would divide into a girl's house at Jane's and a boy's + dogs house at our home. Jane had everything ready for us. Mom had one guest bedroom, and I had another. Jane created a luxurious rehab setting for me. I rested in a luxe private bedroom with an adjoining bathroom. On a king-sized bed with a bank of cushy pillows, I managed to sleep without disturbing the drainage tubes and stitches. The pillows kept me properly positioned. With delicious meals, daily naps, wound care, and pain meds, the days with Jane and my mother's T.L.C. passed, and my strength returned.

Good news from the pathology report capped the week—the breast tissue Dr. G. removed revealed an empty cavity where the tumor had been. The chemo had been more effective than we had dared to hope. I was declared to have had a PCR, "a pathologic complete response." In other words, I was cancer-free for the moment. Mom, Mike, Jane, Tex, and I celebrated with a festive dinner. "We give you thanks, O God, for Jan's successful treatment," Tex said before our meal.

~⌣~

One month post-surgery, a new school year began. I had a full schedule of four classes with three different preparations. I met my students online—sometimes with a cap on and sometimes with my baldness unconcealed. Delicate little curly hairs began to grow on my head. My eyelashes began to return. Even when I could only see my students in the small boxes on my computer screen, and sometimes only see their names in white letters on black rectangles, I was grateful to be back at work. Connecting with my students and reading their words that demonstrated their insightful engagement with the biblical studies and interfaith material I introduced to them was deeply satisfying.

By mid-December, I had completed the semester, presented an academic paper at a conference, and had my reconstructive surgery. The time seemed to fly. The surgery to remove the crunchy plastic "spacers" (which I hated) and to insert permanent silicone implants (which I didn't mind) went well. Now, I was bustier than I had been since my long-ago days of nursing. My young granddaughter pointed to them once. "Boobies!" she announced. I smiled.

"These things are strictly ornamental," I told her.

In all of the treatments' visible side-effects, cancer made me uncomfortably aware of my vanity. I hated losing my eyelashes more than my head of hair. The fact that I weighed more at the end of the year than I had at the beginning of it annoyed me. "Am I the only person who undergoes cancer treatment and doesn't lose any weight, but instead gains a few pounds?" I complained to my oncologist's physician's assistant. She looked at me with mild reproach. "You are very fortunate that this is your concern," she said. "It's much worse for patients who lose a lot of weight." I took her point and silently cursed my vanity. After reconstructive surgery, I joked that my weight gain was entirely due to the implants. "These things must weigh five pounds each!"

I didn't suffer in my breast cancer sojourn. I had a serious medical experience—sometimes intense and often uncomfortable. I became a "survivor." I chose to have all my breast tissue removed. I chose reconstruction. The main side-effects that I experienced in chemo were hair loss and some fatigue. But I didn't get seriously ill.

Doctors detected the disease early and my chemo regime was deftly tailored to my cancer stage and its chemical profile, so my year-long passage from detection through treatment was relatively smooth. I had a loving support system. I had wonderful doctors, nurses, and technicians coordinating to provide me with excellent medical care. I had access to them because I have good health insurance, an incredible privilege in our current health care system in Texas. I was able to pay the extraordinarily high "discounted" cost of each Herceptin injection in a new year with a fresh deductible to meet. My story illustrates the value of medical vigilance and the power of early detection when it comes to breast cancer. I am proof that mammograms and well-woman checkups do save lives.

My breast cancer odyssey—a journey into and through an unfamiliar territory and back home to what passes for my "normal"—was a skillful teacher. Throughout that year, I was sobered by the active realization of my mortality. I was humbled by the great suffering I witnessed all around me. I saw exhaustion on many faces and fear on many others. I observed the courage of good humor despite dire prospects. I stared heartbroken as a visibly pregnant woman walked down the hallway to see her oncologist. I encountered a younger friend wheeling her gaunt, young husband into the oncology center. He would not survive the year. Throughout it all, I had a close-up view of how awful the diagnosis of cancer can be and of its human toll which was nested within the deadly context of the Covid pandemic.

Beyond my encounters with suffering, cancer reconnected me to the deep and robust sustenance of Centering Prayer. I had been attending a small Centering Prayer group meeting since the spring of 2013, but my consistency over the years, in both showing up for these meetings and for my own personal practice, was not great. Centering Prayer practice is a form of Christian meditation that involves silence, stillness, a sacred word on which to focus one's attention, and an openness to the healing, transforming presence of the Divine.

Most Monday nights, our small group would gather in a space made available by a local church, sit in a circle, and center for twenty-five minutes. Then, we would read and discuss a spiritual classic of our choosing. Over the years, the group has grown and contracted, changed and stabilized. Until Covid, my participation had dwindled. When the pandemic forced everything online *and* when I got my diagnosis, I became a regular. Via Zoom, we would share news from our lives, meditate, have our book study, and pray for each other before closing the meeting. These Monday evening sessions became anchoring and sacred times for me and revived my personal commitment to this prayer practice.

Now, I cannot start my day without centering. Each morning, I sit in silence, openness, and quiet attentiveness for at least twenty minutes. An app provides the resonant sound of a singing bowl and keeps the time. Another chime lets me know when the designated time has elapsed. Some sessions fill my heart with spiritual awareness and a keen sense of God's presence. Other sessions are muddled with distractions or just an experience of silence. But, showing up and sitting with the intention of openness is its own reward. My Centering Prayer community and my own practice, along with my beloved church community, have kept me steady in the quest to live a God-ward life and to be an agent of love.

"Are you alone?" Dr. N. had asked.

As I look back across that harrowing cancer year, I can clearly see that I am *not* alone. I am nested within a loving family within a loving community of friends and colleagues and neighbors within a city that is home to exceptional medical facilities within a world that, for all its harsh and hurtful aspects, is filled with natural beauty and seasonal renewal. And I perceive with great clarity that I am held secure within the hands of a loving and sovereign God. Even as I finger the scar left behind by my port, I marvel with gratitude at how my life has been restored to me, and I resolve to honor this gift.

Acknowledgments

To My Twelve Writers:

Why is there a rope on the covers of this book? Because you held on. Sometimes you were holding on for dear life, and other times you were helping someone at the other end of the rope as you tried to pull them out of their uncertainty or sorrow.

I'm so grateful to each of you for your courage, honesty, and hard work. You quickly realized that your story had the power to inspire others; without your agreeing to tell it, this book wouldn't be born.

Leslie Cechan	Julia Williams Dade	Dinah Harris	Linda McDermitt	Tracey McKenzie	Leslie McKinney

Leanne Mertzman	Jan Neece	Jan Quesada	Kristene Ruddle	Kerrin Rummel	Layla Shah

Janis, Scott, and David:

Once again, I couldn't have done this without your support and expertise. I'm extraordinarily blessed to have each of you in my life. Thanks for believing in this project and in me.

Made in the USA
Monee, IL
13 August 2023